W9-BLB-655

LIFE IN CHRIST

Copyright © 1991 Angus Hudson Ltd/
Three's Company
Text copyright © 1979, 1991 John Stott

Unless otherwise stated, all Scripture
quotations in this publication are from the
Holy Bible, New International Version.
Copyright © 1973, 1978, 1984 by
International Bible Society. Published in
North America by Zondervan Corporation.

Designed and created by
Three's Company
5 Dryden Street
London WC2E 9NW

Worldwide co-edition organized and
produced by
Angus Hudson Ltd
Concorde House
Grenville Place
London NW7 3SA
Phone: +44 181 959 3668
Fax: +44 181 959 3678

Designer: Peter M.Wyart
Editor: Tim Dowley

Typesetting by Watermark, Cromer

Printed in Singapore

Published by Baker Books
a division of Baker Book House Company
P.O. Box 6287
Grand Rapids, MI 49516–6287

First printing, 1996

ISBN 0–8010–1128–0

LIFE IN CHRIST

John Stott

Baker Books
A Division of Baker Book House Co
Grand Rapids, Michigan 49516

Contents

Abbreviations

      N.B.   Unless otherwise indicated, the biblical quotations in this
      book are taken from the New International Version (1984).

List of illustrations

Introduction: The Centrality of Christ

Jesus of Nazareth continues to enjoy an extraordinary boom. People are fascinated by him, even in spite of themselves. Many who never reach the point of confessing him as God and Saviour yet regard him with profound admiration. True, there are others who resent and reject him. But the one thing people seem unable to do is to ignore him and leave him alone.

Even in other religions and ideologies Jesus is held in high honour. Hindus would gladly recognize him as an 'avatar' (descent) of Vishnu, and so assimilate him into Hinduism, if only he would renounce his exclusive claims. Jews who reject Jesus as their Messiah have never lost interest in him. Their scholars write books about him, and their hostility has often been more to Gentile antisemitism than to Jesus himself. Moslems acknowledge him as one of·the great prophets, whose virgin birth, sinlessness, miracles, inspiration and future return are all affirmed in the Koran. Marxists, while fiercely critical of 'religion' as an opium which drugs the oppressed into tolerating the injustices of the status quo, nevertheless respect Jesus for his confrontation with the establishment and his compassionate solidarity with the poor.

As T.R.Glover wrote in *The Jesus of History:* 'Jesus remains the very heart and soul of the Christian movement, still controlling men, still capturing men... In fine, there is no figure in human history that signifies more. Men may love him or hate him, but they do it intensely' (SCM 1917; 12th edition 1920, pp.3,5).

My theme in this book is that Jesus Christ is the centre of Christianity, and that therefore both the Christian faith and the Christian life, if they are to be authentic, must be focused on Christ. In his work, *Christian Faith and Other Faiths* the late Bishop Stephen Neill wrote: 'The old saying "Christianity is Christ" is almost exactly true. The historical figure of Jesus of Nazareth is the criterion by which every Christian affirmation has to be judged, and in the light of which it stands or falls' (Oxford University Press 1961, p.91). Professor John Mbiti of Kenya has expressed the same conviction even more succinctly in the words: 'The uniqueness of Christianity is in Jesus Christ' (*African Religions and Philosophy*, Heinemann 1969, p.277).

My third witness is Sundar Singh, who was born into an Indian Sikh family but after his conversion became an itinerant Christian Sadhu. He was once asked by an agnostic professor of comparative religions in a Hindu College what he had found in Christianity which he had not found in his old religion. 'I have Christ,' he replied. 'Yes, I know,' said the professor a little impatiently, 'but what particular principle or doctrine have you found that you did not have before?' 'The particular thing I have found,' he replied, 'is Christ' (*The Christ of the Indian Road* by Stanley Jones, first published 1925, Hodder & Stoughton, 1926, p.64).

I propose, then, to explore the implications of a Christian faith and life which are focused on Christ, and to do so by means of the prepositions which are used in the New Testament in reference to him. In themselves prepositions are insignificant little words, but they can also be signposts to profound theological truths. At all events, many prepositions are pressed into service in the New Testament to portray the richness of a Christian's relation to Christ. We are said to live our lives 'through' Christ, 'on' him, 'in' him, 'under' him, 'for' him, 'with' him, 'unto' him and 'like' him. Our relationship to Christ is thus displayed as a multi-faceted diamond of great beauty.

My purpose is not just theoretical, however, namely that we may come to appreciate more fully the glory of Jesus Christ. It is also pastoral and practical. How can we develop our relationship to him? How can Jesus Christ become more real to us until he occupies the central place in our lives? The process of Christian growth which is implied by these questions is as mysterious in its maturing as falling in love. For as a couple come to know, respect and love one another more and more, until each feels the other to be indispensable, and they agree to marry, so we are to come to know, worship and love Jesus Christ more and more until he becomes indispensable to us, and life without him would be inconceivable.

It will then be possible for us to say:

> Yea, thro' life, death, thro' sorrow and thro' sinning,
>   He shall suffice me, for he hath sufficed.
> Christ is the end, for Christ is the beginning,
>   Christ the beginning, for the end is Christ.
>   St Paul, *by F.W.H.Myers.*

John Stott, 1990

1
Through Christ our Mediator

Anybody who attends a church service for the first time is struck by the shape of our Christian prayers. Almost every petition is addressed to 'Almighty God our Heavenly Father' and ends 'through Jesus Christ our Lord'. Sometimes both the address and the conclusion are more elaborate. One prayer in the 1662 Prayer Book begins 'Almighty and everlasting God' and ends 'Grant this, O Lord, for the honour of our advocate and mediator Jesus Christ'. In another we begin 'Most gracious God' and conclude that all the blessings we have mentioned 'we humbly beg in the name and mediation of Jesus Christ our most blessed Lord and Saviour'.

This common liturgical formula 'through Jesus Christ our Lord' introduces us to the concept of 'mediation'. It echoes Paul's statement that 'there is one God, and there is one mediator between God and men, the man Christ Jesus' (1 Timothy 2:5). It declares, in other words, that God the Father's actions towards humankind have been taken not directly but indirectly, namely through Jesus Christ his Son; and that in consequence our approach to him must be through Jesus Christ our Saviour.

On hearing this, many people are puzzled, and some make no attempt to conceal their impatience. Why should God act, and why should we pray, only through Jesus Christ? they ask. It makes him seem so remote. Prayer becomes like the protocol of a royal or presidential palace, by which one is not allowed to approach the sovereign or president direct, but only through the prescribed court official. It begins to resemble the worst aspects of bureaucracy: you cannot get to the top person with the real authority, but are always fobbed off with some petty civil servant. Why should God behave like that? Why can't he deal with us direct, instead of at one remove? In fact, why is Jesus Christ necessary at all?

I have myself often been asked bewildered questions like these. Other people are more self-confident and roundly disagree with the Bible and with Christian tradition. They by-pass Jesus Christ altogether. They claim to know God, to have a personal relationship with him, and to enjoy mystical experiences, quite apart from Jesus Christ. 'I find Jesus Christ superfluous' some even dare to say.

This, then, is the question we are to pursue in the first chapter of this book. It has been a fundamental conviction of Christians of every church in every generation that we can know and approach God only 'through Jesus Christ his Son our Saviour'; that in this phrase the preposition 'through' expresses something indispensable in our relationship to God; that Jesus Christ's mediation, far from being responsible for the remoteness of God, actually overcomes it; and that through Jesus Christ Almighty God comes near to us, bringing us a clearer understanding and a closer relationship than would be possible in any other way. 'Through Jesus Christ' means access to God, not barriers. It indicates the only bridge over an otherwise unbridgeable chasm.

The gulf between God and us

The proper place to begin, therefore, is with the nature of this chasm. Only when we grasp how wide it is, shall we be ready to acknowledge the inadequacy of our own bridges and the indispensability of Jesus Christ.

First, there is the gulf between us as finite creatures and God our infinite Creator. In one sense, the relation between the Creator and his human creatures is one of similarity rather than dissimilarity, because God has made us in his own image. As a result, we can perceive something of his rationality through our ability to reason, something of his love through our loving, something of his holiness through the moral law he has written in our hearts. Yet the gulf remains between Creator and creatures, between the Infinite and the finite. We sigh with Job: 'If only I knew where to find him; if only I could go to his dwelling!' (Job 23:3). Instinctively we know that we cannot box God up in any conceptual framework of our own devising, and that if we think we have succeeded in doing so, then what we have in our box is not God. Our little minds cannot conceive him, let alone contain him. '"For my thoughts are not your thoughts, neither are your ways my ways" declares the Lord. "As the heavens are higher than the earth, so are my ways higher than your ways and my thoughts than your thoughts"' (Isaiah 55:8, 9).

Even the fleeting glimpses we catch of him as he passes by in moments of ecstasy or pain, of beauty or wonder, of goodness or love, leave us tantalized by the fulness of the Reality beyond. Yet these glimpses are themselves a form of 'mediation'. For they are declarations of God through the glories of heaven and earth, through the intricate mechanisms of nature, through the complexities of the human situation in its combination of nobility and degradation, and through the whole range of our responses to it. These 'mediations' leave us dissatisfied, however. They point to heights we cannot scale, to depths we cannot fathom. We need a mediation that is at once more concrete, more personal, more genuinely human. In a word, we need Jesus Christ. For however rich the reality we have ever seen or felt or thought or suspected, apart from Jesus Christ, God remains the Infinitely Beyond. Only once has this Beyond come personally into our midst, when the Eternal Word of God actually became a human being and lived among us. Only then did human eyes behold true 'glory' in human form, the radiance of ultimate personal reality, 'the glory of the One and Only, who came from the Father' (John 1:14).

The gulf between God and us is still wider than we have so far considered. It is the chasm that yawns between us as rebellious creatures and God our righteous Judge. For the unpalatable truth is that we have defied our Creator, rejected his authority, rebuffed his love and gone our own selfish way. The intractable problems of the world bear witness to this human alienation from God. It is not only that we lack the mental equipment to conceive him, but that we lack the moral integrity to approach him. We are unable to find God by ourselves. Worse, we are unfit to do so. So the kind of mediation we need is even greater than we first thought. It is not just a personal disclosure of God, a making known to us in intelligible form of him who would otherwise remain for ever unknown. It is more, much more, than this. We need 'grace', the free initiative of a merciful God who comes to his rebel creatures not to judge but to save them, not to destroy but to re-create them. And when we are talking about such a gracious initiative of God, as when we are talking about a personal disclosure of God, we are talking about Jesus Christ. For 'Here is a trustworthy saying that deserves full acceptance: Christ Jesus came into the world to save sinners' (1 Timothy 1:15).

Apart from Jesus Christ, then, the chasm between God and us is impassable. It is our human finitude on the one hand, and our self-centred rebellion on the other. By ourselves we can neither know God nor reach him. The pathetic little bridges we build from our side all fall into the abyss. Only one bridge spans the otherwise unbridgeable gulf. It has been thrown across from the other side. It is Jesus Christ, God's eternal Son, who entered our world, became a human being, lived our life, and then died our death, the death we deserved to die because of our sins. But this is to anticipate.

Here is how the unknown author of the so called Letter to the Hebrews expresses at the beginning of his treatise the unique ministry of Jesus Christ:

In the past God spoke to our forefathers through the prophets at many times and in various ways, ²but in these last days he has spoken to us by his Son, whom he appointed heir of all things, and through whom he made the universe. ³The Son is the radiance of God's glory and the exact representation of his being, sustaining all things by his powerful word. After he had provided purification for sins, he sat down at the right hand of the Majesty in heaven. ⁴So he became as much superior to the angels as the name he has inherited is superior to theirs. (Hebrews 1:1–4)

The majesty of this early witness to Jesus Christ ranks with John's in the prologue to his Gospel (John 1:1–14) and with Paul's in his Letter to the Colossians (Colossians 1:15–23). It brings together the two major spheres of mediation, in which God has taken action through Jesus Christ, which we usually call 'revelation' and 'redemption'. That is, God has both spoken to our ignorance through Jesus Christ, and dealt with our sins through Jesus Christ.

Moreover, in both spheres Jesus Christ is supreme and has no rivals. This, in fact, is the theme of the Letter to the Hebrews. Its readers were Jewish Christians who were being persecuted for their faith in Jesus and were on that account in danger of renouncing their Christianity and lapsing into Judaism. But how could they possibly turn back from the fulfilment to the anticipation, from the reality to the shadow? It could only be that they had never seen Jesus as he is. So the writer set himself to demonstrate the superiority of Jesus Christ to all Old Testament figures, indeed his supremacy over all who had gone before or could come after. Thus, in the sphere of revelation Jesus was a prophet greater than Moses, and in the sphere of redemption he was a priest greater than Aaron. For through Jesus Christ we know God more fully than was possible through the teaching of Moses, and through Jesus Christ we approach God more intimately than was possible through the priesthood of Aaron.

God's revelation through Jesus Christ

The writer draws a contrast between the Old and New Testaments. What is common to both is that *God spoke*. 'In the past God spoke to our forefathers through the prophets' (verse 1), but 'in these last days he has spoken to us by his Son' (verse 2). The same verb in the same aorist tense occurs twice.

Now this assertion that God has 'spoken', that he has put his thoughts into words, must be taken with full seriousness. It is impossible for us human beings to read even each other's thoughts if we remain silent. Only if I speak to you can you know what is in my mind; only if you speak to me can I know what is in your mind. If, then, men and women remain strangers to each other until and unless they speak to one another, how much more will God remain a stranger to us unless he speaks or has spoken? His thoughts are not our thoughts, as we have seen. It is impossible for human beings to read the mind of God. If we are ever to know his mind he must speak; he must clothe his thoughts in words. This, we believe, is precisely what he has done. In Old Testament days he spoke through the prophets, and now in

these last days he has spoken through his Son.

But if the fact of the divine speech is the same in both Testaments, the time, the mode and the contents of God's revelation are different.

As for the *time*, he spoke 'in the past to our forefathers', while now he has spoken 'in these last days to us'. 'These last days' is a phrase expressing the apostles' conviction that the long expected new age arrived with Jesus and that we are now living in the final period of history, while the 'us' to whom God has now spoken refers to the new international community of every class and culture which Jesus Christ has founded. There is therefore both a finality and a universality about the revelation of God through Jesus Christ.

As for the *mode* of revelation God spoke to our forefathers through the prophets 'in various ways', whereas he has now spoken to us 'by his Son'. The process of prophetic inspiration was indeed extremely diverse. Occasionally God revealed himself through visions, dreams and trance-like experiences, but more often by oracular utterances in which 'the word of the Lord came' to the prophets and through them to the people. More often still, since the whole of the Old Testament was regarded as in some sense 'prophetic', the writers were in full possession of their faculties, as when they were writing historical narrative or psalms, proverbs and other kinds of wisdom literature. These are some of the ways in which God spoke in Old Testament times. But now God has spoken 'by his Son', which means not only through the teaching of Jesus of Nazareth but also and especially through his person and his deeds, for in these the glory of God was seen.

As for the *content* of the revelation, the 'many times and various ways' of Hebrews 1 verse 1 could be more literally translated 'in many parts and in many ways'. In other words, the self-disclosure of God through the Old Testament was not only varied in form, but also partial in content. Christians believe in progressive revelation, that God revealed himself bit by bit and stage by stage, each new stage building on those which had preceded it. But over against the 'many parts' of the Old Testament revelation is set God's Son who, it is implied, is the grand finale of the drama, since in and through him God's self-disclosure was brought to completion.

This completeness is emphasized by the greatness of the Person through whom the revelation was made. He is given the highest imaginable descriptive titles, in relation first to the universe and then to God himself. In relation to the universe he is called the 'heir of all things', the agent 'through whom he [God] made the universe' (verse 2) and the one who is meanwhile 'sustaining all things by his powerful word' (verse 3). Thus by three deceptively simple expressions the writer moves from the beginning of history through all its unfolding to its climax, and claims that the whole universe was created through the agency of Jesus Christ God's Son in the first place, is now sustained by his powerful word and will one day be received by him as his rightful inheritance.

In relation to God he is first called 'Son', an 'excellent name' or exalted title which (as the writer goes on to demonstrate at length, verses 4 to 14) is given to no angel. Next 'he is the radiance of God's glory and the exact representation of his being' (verse 3). Both these expressions are forceful figures of speech. They are taken on the one hand from the outdoor world of sunshine and on the other from the indoor world of documents, wax and seals. And both express, in so far as human words and images can express, the relation of the Son to the Father in the eternal mystery of the Godhead. According to the first, the Son is 'the radiance of God's glory', like the sunlight streaming continuously from the sun, or in the words of the Nicene Creed 'light from light'. According to the second, the Son is 'the exact representation' of the Father's being, like the impress made by a seal on wax. Together, the two expressions complement one another, the sunlight picture emphasizing the Son's oneness with the Father, and the picture of the seal's impress on wax his distinctness from the Father. Both were of great importance when the theologians of the fourth and fifth centuries were seeking to define the nature of the Son's relation to the Father over against the heretics. The 'Modalists' made him out to be the same person as the Father though now in a different mode, that is, God ceased to be the Father and became the Son. The Arians on the other hand taught that he was a totally distinct person from the Father, indeed created by and therefore subordinate to him. In contrast to these heresies, the Son is described here as being at the same time and eternally one in being with the Father ('the radiance of God's glory') and distinct in 'person' or mode of being from the Father ('the exact representation of his being').

It is this glorious and unique Person – Son, radiance and image of the Father, creator, upholder and heir of the universe – who took 'flesh and blood' like us (Hebrews 2:14), experienced our sufferings and our temptations (Hebrews 2:10,18), and tasted death for us (Hebrews 2:9,14). Thus he who was really God became really and truly man. Because he became man we can understand him, for we see him in the human context with which we are familiar. Because he was also God, however, what we see within his humanity is nothing less than a disclosure of the being and purpose of God. He calls God his Father, and authorizes, indeed encourages, us to do the same. He speaks of God's Kingdom or rule, and urges us to 'believe' the good news of its arrival, to 'receive' it ourselves, and to 'seek' it as our chief ambition by setting its growth before us as the supreme good to which we devote our lives. We see his power over nature as he stills storms, walks on water, multiplies loaves and fish, heals diseases and reclaims people from death. We observe his reverent submission to the authority of Old Testament Scripture, his penetrating insight into its fundamental principles, and his decisive rejection of all human traditions which contradict or confuse it. We watch him treating women and children with honour, having compassion on the poor and the despised, feeding the hungry and forgiving the sinful. We hear him 'snorting' with indignation in the presence of death, commanding the demons to go and expressing woes and warnings against hypocrites. We see him setting his face like a rock towards Jerusalem, refusing to be deflected from the path of suffering which had been written of him, experiencing agony in the garden and God-forsakenness on the Cross. And then we see him again as the Risen Lord, who has secured salvation for sinners and conquered death, and who now claims universal authority and commissions his followers to go and make all nations his disciples.

Through all this and much more we behold his glory, and recognize it as the glory of God's only Son. He is 'full of grace and truth', of power and gentleness, of compassion to the humble and severity to the proud, of righteousness, faith and love. And as we watch him, his attitudes and actions mirror the Father's. To be sure, when some people talk about God, they oblige us to be atheists. 'I do not believe in God', we have to affirm, 'or at least not in the God you seem to believe in'. But when we see and hear Jesus, our response is entirely different. 'This is the God we believe in', we say, the living and true God, the God revealed through Jesus Christ. For 'we know that the Son of God has come, and has given us understanding so that we may know him who is true' (1 John 5:20). As Jesus himself is recorded as having said to Philip, 'anyone who has seen me has seen the Father' (John 14:9).

God's redemption through Jesus Christ

Jesus came not only to teach but to save, not only to reveal God to human beings, but also to redeem human beings for God. This is because our major problem is not our ignorance but our sin and guilt. And the redemption which God has achieved, like the revelation which he has given, is 'through Jesus Christ'. Jesus Christ is the agent or mediator of both.

The way this is expressed in the Letter to the Hebrews is that he 'provided purification for sins' (Hebrews 1:3). The language is borrowed from the Old Testament sacrificial system. In the rest of Hebrews Jesus is portrayed as our 'great high priest', greater than Aaron, who offered the perfect sacrifice for sin. This was neither a bull, nor a goat, nor a lamb, but himself. The sacrifice of animals in the Old Testament was only a shadow of the reality to come, namely Christ's shedding of his own blood, his laying down his life for us. Indeed, the writer to the Hebrews goes further and boldly applies to Jesus the symbolism of the scape-goat, when he declares that he was 'offered once to bear the sins of many' (Hebrews 9:28, RSV). This 'better sacrifice' is the basis of the 'better promises' of the 'better covenant' (Hebrews 7:22; 8:6; 9:23). For 'it is impossible for the blood of bulls and goats to take away sins' (Hebrews 10:4). Now, however, that Jesus Christ has shed his own 'blood of the new covenant...for the forgiveness of sins', as he said he would (Matthew 26:28), God's New Covenant promise is in force: 'I will remember their sins no more' (Hebrews 8:7–13; 10:15–18).

The author of Hebrews makes much of this great promise that God will never bring to mind again the sins which he has forgiven. It is a finished forgiveness of sins made possible only by a finished sacrifice for sins. And this the writer sees vividly symbolized in the sitting posture of Jesus. He draws attention to it at the beginning of his letter: 'After he had provided purification for sins, he sat down at the right hand of the Majesty in heaven' (Hebrews 1:3). He elaborates it later: 'Day after day every priest stands and performs his religious duties; again and again he offers the same sacrifices, which can never take away sins. But when this priest had offered for all time one single sacrifice for sins, he sat down at the right hand of God' (Hebrews 10:11,12). No seats were in fact provided for the priests in the tabernacle or in the temple. They stood to minister because their task was never done. Day after day, week after week, month after month, year after year, they continued their interminable ministry and offered their endless sacrifices. Then at last the Great High Priest Jesus came, 'offered for all time one sacrifice for sins' and sat down. This is the 'one oblation of himself once offered' and the 'full, perfect and sufficient sacrifice, oblation and satisfaction for the sins of the whole world' which Cranmer so triumphantly celebrated in his 1662 Holy Communion service. The Old Testament priests stood because their work was unfinished; he sat because his work was done. For 'by one sacrifice he has made perfect for ever those who are being made holy' (Hebrews 10:14).

As a result of the unique priesthood and perfect sacrifice of Jesus, to whom we have fled for refuge and through whom we have received a complete forgiveness, we may now constantly draw near to God. In Old Testament days only the priests might draw near. Through the veil into the very presence of God in the Most Holy Place, only the high priest might come, and then only once a year on the Day of Atonement. All others had to keep their distance, on pain of death. But now this distinction between priest and people has been abolished by Jesus. Now there is a 'priesthood of all believers'. For now through him all may draw near, pastors and people, sovereign and commoners, without any discrimination whatever. So the writer to the Hebrews exhorts his readers to avail themselves of their privileged access to God: 'Therefore, brothers, since we have confidence to enter the Most Holy Place by the blood of Jesus, by a new and living way opened for us through the curtain, that is, his body, and since we have a great priest over the house of God, let us draw near to God with a sincere heart in full assurance of faith, having our hearts sprinkled to cleanse us from a guilty conscience and having our bodies washed with pure water' (Hebrews 10:19–22). This 'full assurance of faith' is just what many modern Christians seem to lack. They are shy and timid in their approach to God and uncertain of themselves. They declare that they are unworthy to draw near. Of course they are! None of us has any worthiness which qualifies us to draw near. But what about the worthiness of Jesus Christ and of his perfect sacrifice for sin? It is through him alone that we may and must draw near. You see, then, that a true doctrine of the mediation of Jesus Christ is the ground of Christian assurance. Only when we come to God through Jesus Christ who died for us can we come with boldness instead of timidity, with confidence instead of fear. Notice too, as was mentioned earlier, that the concept of Jesus Christ as mediator, far from keeping us remote from God, is the very means by which we may approach him.

The apostle Paul emphasizes the same truth and expresses the same assurance in his Letter to the Romans. For, having demonstrated that all human beings are guilty before God, and having explained God's way of putting sinners right with himself, which is not on the basis of their own works but of Christ's self-sacrifice for our sins, when we put our trust in him, he goes on: 'Therefore, since we have been justified through faith, we have peace with God through our Lord Jesus Christ through whom we have gained access by faith into this grace in which we now stand...When we were God's enemies, we were reconciled to him through the death of his Son...We also rejoice in God through our Lord Jesus Christ, through whom we have now received reconciliation' (Romans 5:1,2,10,11). Five times in this one brief paragraph Paul repeats the preposition 'through' in relation to Jesus Christ. It is through the death of Christ that we were reconciled to God. So it is through Christ that we have received our reconciliation, that we have obtained access into the state of grace, that we enjoy peace with God, and that we rejoice in God. Reconciliation, access, peace and joy – these are all blessings which become ours only through the finished sacrifice and the present mediation of Jesus Christ. No wonder our prayers are offered to God through him, for there is no other way to the Father except through his Son, our Lord and Saviour, Jesus Christ (John 14:6).

Everything begins with God the Father. The initiative of grace is his alone. It is he who in sheer love desired both to show himself to us (which is 'revelation') and to bring us to himself (which is 'redemption').

In both he acted through Jesus Christ. It is through Christ that he has revealed himself to us, and it is through Christ that he has redeemed us for himself.

Moreover, God's revelation and redemption through Jesus

Christ are both complete. The writer to the Hebrews is emphatic about this. It is 'in these last days', he says, that God has spoken to us through his Son, and then, after the Son had made purification for sins, 'he sat down' (Hebrews 1:2,3). There is about both a historical finality.

It is inconceivable, therefore, that there could ever be either a higher revelation than God has given through the person of Jesus Christ his Son, or a fuller redemption than he has achieved through the work of Jesus Christ our Saviour. Both are perfect and complete. What God said and did through Jesus Christ he did *hapax*, 'once and for all'. This is a favourite word in Hebrews with reference to the Cross (Hebrews 7:27; 9:12, 26–28; 10:10; see also Romans 6:10 and 1 Peter 3:18) and is also used by Jude of 'the faith that was once for all entrusted to the saints' (Jude 3). Thus, Christ was offered for our sins once for all, and the faith has been delivered to us once and for all. Please do not misunderstand these affirmations. They do not of course mean that either our understanding of God or our relationship to God is perfect, but rather that what God has done to make these possible, namely his revelation and redemption through Jesus, are perfect. We have much more to learn, but God has no more to reveal than he has revealed in Jesus Christ. Therefore we shall grow in our Christian understanding as the Holy Spirit enlightens our minds to perceive more of the glory which God has once and for all revealed in Jesus Christ. Again, we have much more to receive, but God has no more to give than he has given in Jesus Christ. Therefore we shall grow in our Christian character as the Holy Spirit enables us to claim more of the spiritual inheritance which God has once for all given us in Jesus Christ.

Hence the emphasis of the sixteenth century Reformers on *sola scriptura* (Scripture alone for our authority) and *sola gratia* (grace alone for our salvation). Hence too the contemporary evangelical emphasis on the Bible and the Cross, and on the finality of both. It is not because we are ultra-conservative, or obscurantist, or reactionary or other horrid things which we are sometimes said to be. It is rather because we love Jesus Christ, and because we are determined, God helping us, to bear witness to his unique glory and absolute sufficiency. In Christ and in the biblical witness to Christ God's revelation is complete; to add any words of our own to this finished word is derogatory to Christ. In Christ and in his atoning work on the Cross God's redemption is complete; to add any works of our own to this finished work is derogatory to Christ. This is how we see it. It is a question of Christ's honour, and it is all implied in the first preposition we have considered. For whatever we know of God we know through Jesus Christ, and whatever we have received from God we have received through Jesus Christ. So praise be to God through Jesus Christ our Lord!

2
On Christ
our Foundation

Every architect and builder knows the importance of stable foundations. A good building with bad foundations is worse than useless; it is positively dangerous.

Our church family at All Souls, Langham Place, London, has recently gained fresh insight into this fact. For when John Nash began to build the church in 1822, he encountered an unexpected problem. The site, which is thought to have been an old brick yard, was found to be full of drains and cesspools. Reporting this to the Commissioners, he told them that if they wanted to ensure sound foundations, they would have to spend a further £1,800, which represented about 10 per cent of the total cost of erection. Until a few years ago this was no more than a piece of historical information. But now it assumed a new importance. We had become increasingly dissatisfied with the building. Despite its beauty, it was unsuited to modern needs. Visibility and audibility were both poor. People in the galleries felt themselves cut off from the worship and reduced to the status of spectators. There was no flexibility in the chancel to permit the use of drama or to accommodate the orchestra. There was little or no sense of being 'gathered round the action'. And there was neither hall, nor dining room, nor kitchen to make possible the serving of meals and the development of fellowship. How could the church building be restructured to remedy its defects and supply its missing facilities? Could a hall be constructed underneath in such a way that at the same time the church floor could be raised and the interior redesigned? Robert Potter, who was appointed architect for the proposed reconstruction, probed John Nash's foundations. His first discovery was that 'there was sufficient depth to permit the formation of a great crypt extending beneath the whole of the church' (*Inside Story*, the building project of All Souls Church, Langham Place, London, 1976, p. 17). Because of the marshy soil John Nash had sunk his foundations at least three feet below the level he had originally intended. The second discovery was that Nash had taken

'exceptional precautions to ensure that the weight of the building
was evenly distributed, by constructing inverted arches spanning
the supports to the piers'. These 'very interesting brickwork arches,
which are of exceptional quality for foundations' Mr Potter has
skilfully incorporated into his design for the basement hall.

In a letter dated October 1978 Robert Potter kindly explained to
me something of the theory which controls foundations, namely the
need for the force of gravity to be balanced by an equal and opposite
force, if resistance to compression is to be adequate. In contrast to
Nash's sound construction in the Regency period, he went on to
instance medieval builders who were less wise: 'At Chichester
Bishop Ralph de Luffa's Cathedral, a massive simple Romanesque
building, with no piers or point loads, was founded upon the
remains of a Roman city. Over the centuries the made ground, con-
sisting of débris and burials dating from the Roman era and shortly
before, has compressed and disrupted the superstructure, so that my
first task as Surveyor in 1962 was to reinforce the foundations. We
discovered that if Bishop Ralph had extended his footings by
another 4′ 6″ this would have been unnecessary.'

If the stability of buildings depends largely on their foundations,
so does the stability of human lives. The search for personal security
is a primal instinct, but many fail to find it today. Old familiar land-
marks are being obliterated. Moral absolutes which were once
thought to be eternal are being abandoned. Many feel like the psal-
mist when wickedness increased and people taunted him saying:
'when the foundations are being destroyed, what can the righteous
do?' (Psalm 11:3). In such circumstances, when like Abraham we
recognize that we are no more than pilgrims or nomads on earth, it
is natural to look forward 'to the city with foundations, whose
architect and builder is God' and to cling to those things which
remain firm and 'cannot be shaken' (Hebrews 11:10; 12:26–28).

In particular, Christians have always thought of Jesus Christ as
the only solid foundation on which to rest their souls and build their
lives. Many of the great hymns of the church celebrate this truth.
There is, for example, the old Latin hymn dating from the seventh
or eighth century. The most familiar translation begins:

> Christ is our cornerstone
> On him alone we build.

Less well known is J. M. Neale's rendering:

> Christ is made the sure foundation,
>   Christ the head and corner-stone,
> Chosen of the Lord, and precious,
>   Binding all the church in one,
> Holy Sion's help for ever,
>   And her confidence alone.

The same concept was expressed in more personal terms by John Newton. Once a godless sailor and slave trader, who was then wonderfully converted during a storm at sea, he had good cause to write 'Amazing grace, how sweet the sound'. He also wrote:

> How sweet the name of Jesus sounds
>> In a believer's ear!
> It soothes his sorrows, heals his wounds,
>> And drives away his fear.
>
> Dear name, the rock on which I build,
>> My shield and hiding place;
> My never-failing treasury, filled
>> With boundless stores of grace.

I have myself been struck by the large number of New Testament passages in which the preposition 'on' (*epi*) is used in reference to Jesus. Each depicts him as being in some sense the ground on which we stand, the support on which we rely or the foundation on which we build. It is the nature of this relationship which we must investigate. It follows naturally from the first chapter. For if God's initiative of grace has been taken 'through' Christ, the preposition 'on' describes our response. God has acted through Jesus Christ, and we rest upon what he has done. God has spoken through Jesus Christ, and we build our lives upon this unique revelation.

Resting on the work of Christ

We saw in the last chapter that, having borne our sins on the Cross and thus offered a 'full, perfect and sufficient sacrifice...for the sins of the whole world', Jesus Christ sat down at the Father's right hand. For his atoning work is finished, his deed of salvation is done. There is no need for us to add anything to it. Indeed, to attempt to do so is to cast doubt on the satisfactoriness of what he did.

Therefore, if Christ is 'resting' from his work, having finished it, we should be 'resting' in or on it, depending on him alone for our acceptance with God. The Letter to the Hebrews, which emphasizes the sitting posture of Christ in heaven, also makes much of the Christian's rest of faith (Hebrews 3, 4). The writer takes up two Old Testament expressions. One is that 'on the seventh day God... rested from all his work' (Genesis 2:2), and the other is his solemn warning to unbelieving Israel 'they shall never enter my rest' (Psalm 95:11). From these texts the author rightly deduces that there is a 'rest' which God still promises to his people and which becomes ours when we put our trust in Jesus Christ. For 'we who have believed enter that rest' (Hebrews 4:3). He calls it the 'sabbath-rest for the people of God' (Hebrews 4:9), and adds that 'anyone who enters God's rest also rests from his own work, just as God did from his' (Hebrews 4:10). This is a very telling expression. Work and rest exclude one another. If we are working for our salvation, we are not at rest, but if we are resting in Christ's finished work, then we are also resting from those feverish works we used to do to try to win God's favour.

Saving faith is resting faith, the trust which relies entirely on the Saviour. John Paton is said to have learned this when he was translating the Gospel of John. Born in 1824 into a humble Scottish home in Dumfriesshire, John Paton seems to have followed Jesus Christ from his early boyhood. Before studying theology and medicine at university, he served for ten years as a Glasgow City Missionary. Then after graduating he was ordained, and set sail for the New Hebrides as a Presbyterian missionary. Within three months of his arrival on the island of Tanna his young wife died, followed by their five-week-old son. For three more years he laboured alone among the hostile Tannese, ignoring their threats and seeking to make Jesus Christ known to them, before escaping with his life and later spending fifteen years on the island of Aniwa. It is said that he was working one day in his home at the translation of John's Gospel. He was puzzling over the evangelist's favourite expression *pisteuo eis*, to 'believe in' or 'trust in' Jesus Christ, which occurs first in the Gospel's twelfth verse. How could he translate it? The islanders were cannibals. Nobody trusted anybody else. There was no word for 'trust' in their language. His native servant came in. 'What am I doing?' he asked. The man replied that he was sitting at his desk. Paton then raised both his feet off the floor and sat back on his chair. 'What am I doing now?' In reply the servant used a verb which means 'to lean your whole weight upon', and this is the expression Paton used throughout the Gospel to translate 'to believe in'. (For Paton's life see *John G. Paton, Missionary to the New Hebrides*, an autobiography edited by his brother James Paton, Hodder and Stoughton, 1889. The autobiography does not contain the translation story, however, and the British and Foreign Bible Society have been unable to verify it.)

Paton's translation is quite legitimate. Indeed, it is interesting that John's *pisteuo eis* ('to believe into or onto') is several times replaced in Luke's Acts by *pisteuo epi* ('believe on'). For example, in answer to the Philippian jailor's anxious question 'what must I do to be saved?' Paul replied (literally): 'Believe on the Lord Jesus, and you will be saved' (Acts 16:31 cf 9:42; 11:17; 22:19).

There is an urgent need in today's church for a clear understanding of this. For many are spiritually restless and anxious, and lack any assurance of salvation. Some even teach that Christian assurance is a particularly horrid kind of presumption. They overlook John's clear statement that he wrote his first letter to believers with the express intention that they might 'know' they had received eternal life (1 John 5:13). No, true assurance is not presumption. It is rather a 'full assurance of faith' (Hebrews 10:22), the quiet and humble confidence which God gives to all who have repented of being Pharisees, relying on themselves that they are righteous (Luke 18:9, *epi* again), and instead like the publican in the parable have come to rely entirely on the mercy of God revealed in the Cross of Christ.

The real secret of faith's power lies not in the faith itself but in its object, Jesus Christ. As Luther put it in his great commentary on Galatians: 'faith...apprehendeth nothing else but that precious jewel Christ Jesus' (*Commentary on St Paul's Epistle to the Galatians*, 1531; James Clarke, 1953, p.100).

Already in Old Testament days God was teaching his people about alternative objects of faith, especially through Isaiah. In the eighth century BC, before Samaria had fallen, and while the Assyrian peril loomed large on the north-eastern horizon, the civic leaders of Judah were flirting with an Egyptian military alliance. The prophet was incensed by their unbelief and was given woes to pronounce against them. The King of Assyria was quite right to say to them later: 'On what are you basing this confidence of yours?...On whom are you depending...? Look now, you are depending on Egypt, that splintered reed of a staff, which pierces a man's hand and wounds him if he leans on it! Such is Pharaoh king of Egypt to all who depend on him' (2 Kings 18:19–21 and Isaiah 36:4–6). What should they rely on, then, in the national emergency? Here is Isaiah's reply: 'This is what the Sovereign LORD says: "See, I lay a stone in Zion, a precious cornerstone for a sure foundation; the one who trusts will never be dismayed"' (Isaiah 28:16). By this foundation stone, on which God's people should be resting, Isaiah seems to have been referring to the Davidic monarchy, historically at that time represented by good King Hezekiah, but one day to be fulfilled in Jesus Christ.

Isaiah's call to faith became a popular text in the early church. Both Peter and Paul quote it, both apply it to Jesus Christ, and both link it with those other verses in Isaiah about 'a stone that causes men to stumble and a rock that makes them fall' (Isaiah 8:14, 15). Together the two texts point out the alternatives. Jesus Christ is to everybody either a foundation stone or a stumbling-stone. He is God's rock. Either we build our lives on him, or we bark our shins against him, stumble and fall. It is the alternative between the attempt at self-salvation and salvation by Christ's grace alone.

Jewish unbelievers, Paul writes, have 'stumbled over the stumbling-stone'. For, 'since they did not know the righteousness that comes from God, and sought to establish their own, they did not submit to God's righteousness.' Gentiles, on the other hand, who humbled themselves and put their trust not in themselves but exclusively in Christ as Saviour, experienced the truth of the Scripture:

'"Anyone who trusts in him will never be put to shame." For there is no difference between Jew and Gentile – the same Lord is Lord of all and richly blesses all who call on him, for, "Everyone who calls on the name of the Lord will be saved"' (Romans 9:30–10:13).

Relying on the promises of Christ

Humble, confident Christian reliance on Christ as our foundation, however, is reliance on his word as well as on his work, that is to say, on the unbreakable promises which he addresses to those who trust in him.

> How firm a foundation, you people of God,
> is laid for your faith in his excellent word!
> What more can he say to you than he has said
> to everyone trusting in Jesus our head?
>
> Since Jesus is with you, do not be afraid;
> since he is your Lord, you need not be dismayed:
> he strengthens you, guards you, and helps you to stand,
> upheld by his righteous, omnipotent hand.
>
> Whoever has come to believe in his name
> will not be deserted, and not put to shame;
> though hell may endeavour that Christian to shake
> his Lord will not leave him, nor ever forsake.

> Richard Keen (c.1787)
> © in this version *Jubilate Hymns*

I sometimes wonder if there is any more vital lesson for Christian living than this: that God has condescended to our weakness by making us promises, that he will never break them, and that faith reckons on his faithfulness by grasping hold of them. We sometimes smile at the Victorians' 'promise-boxes'. Biblical promises were printed on small pieces of paper, rolled up like miniature scrolls and stored in a wooden box for random selection in times of need. And, to be sure, that practice did wrench the divine promises from the context in which they were originally given. Nevertheless, I rather think that even such a naive trust in detached promises was better than the present-day accurate but unbelieving knowledge of the promises in their context. So many of us complain of spiritual doubt, darkness, depression and lethargy, of besetting sins and unconquered temptations, of slow progress towards Christian maturity, of sluggishness in worship and in prayer, and of many other spiritual ills, while all the time we do not use the secret weapon which God has put into our hands. What this is nobody has illustrated more vividly than Bunyan in his classic *Pilgrim's Progress*.

Christian and Hopeful found themselves in the grounds of Doubting Castle, whose owner was Giant Despair. He found them asleep, and so 'put them into his castle, in a very dark dungeon, nasty and stinking to the spirits of these two men'. 'Here, then, they lay from Wednesday morning till Saturday night, without one bit of bread, or drop of drink, or light, or any to ask how they did.' The first morning, at his wife's instigation, Giant took 'a grievous crab-tree cudgel' and 'fell upon them and beat them fearfully'. The next day his wife advised him 'to counsel them to make away with themselves', which he did, 'either with knife, halter or poison', since they were never likely to escape. On the third day he took them into the castleyard and showed them the gruesome bones and skulls of victims he had killed. 'These,' said he, 'were pilgrims, as you are, once, and they trespassed on my grounds, as you have done; and when I saw fit, I tore them in pieces; and so within ten days I will do you. Get you to your den again...'. All that day they lay there 'in a lamentable case, as before'.

Then about midnight 'they began to pray, and continued in prayer till almost break of day'. A little before dawn came the answer to their prayers. Christian 'brake out into this passionate speech': 'what a fool, quoth he, am I, thus to lie in a stinking dungeon, when I may as well walk in liberty! I have a key in my bosom called Promise that will, I am persuaded, open any lock in Doubting Castle. Then said Hopeful, That's good news, good brother, pluck it out of thy bosom, and try'. So he did, and 'the door flew open with ease', and then the outer door, and then the iron gate, enabling them to escape with speed. Awakened by the creaking of the gate, Giant Despair rose to pursue them, but he 'felt his limbs to fail, for his fits took him again, so that he could by no means go after them' (*Pilgrim's Progress* 1678 and 1684, Collins Classics Edition, 1953, pp. 126–131).

Not only has God made promises in his word, but he has pledged himself to his people by an everlasting covenant. This covenant he ratified by the blood of Christ, guarantees by his own 'steadfast love which endures for ever', and renews to us each time we come to the Holy Communion, which is a solemn covenant sign. With these foundations for faith we really have no excuse for our faithlessness. Edward Mote, Baptist pastor in Horsham, Sussex, for twenty-six years in the middle of the last century, had clearly grasped these truths. One of his best hymns, which Bishop E. H. Bickersteth once called a 'grand hymn of faith', he entitled 'The Immutable Basis of a Sinner's Hope'. You will see that this basis is compounded of the righteousness, death, name or character, grace, covenant and promise of Jesus Christ. With such a solid sixfold foundation, what is there to fear?

My hope is built on nothing less
than Jesus' blood and righteousness;
no merit of my own I claim,
but wholly trust in Jesus' name.
  On Christ,the solid rock, I stand –
  all other ground is sinking sand.

When weary in this earthly race,
I rest on his unchanging grace;
in every wild and stormy gale
my anchor holds and will not fail.

His vow, his covenant and blood
are my defence against the flood;
when earthly hopes are swept away
he will uphold me on that day.

When the last trumpet's voice shall sound,
O may I then in him be found!
clothed in his righteousness alone,
faultless to stand before his throne.
  On Christ, the solid rock, I stand –
  all other ground is sinking sand.

E. Mote (1797–1874)
© in this version *Jubilate Hymns*

Building on the teaching of Christ

Edward Mote's distinction between foundations of rock and sand
goes back to the teaching of Jesus himself. For he concluded his so-
called Sermon on the Mount with the graphic little parable of two
housebuilders who constructed their homes respectively on rock
and sand. When the houses were completed and occupied, they may
well have looked exactly alike. In size, shape and outward decora-
tion there may have been nothing to choose between them. For their
only difference lay in their foundations, and these of course were
hidden from view. At least they were hidden until the fatal day of the
storm. That day, as in Noah's flood, 'all the springs of the great deep
burst forth and the floodgates of the heavens were opened' (Genesis
7:11). The rain fell, the floods rose, and the wind blew. The house
on the rock could not be shaken by the gale; it stood firm. But the
house on sand collapsed in irretrievable ruin (Matthew 7:24–27;
Luke 6:47–49).

Jesus evidently knew what he was talking about. Engineers today
may understand better than he the scientific principles of safe and
stable construction, but they have nothing to add to his insistence

Jesus washing Peter's feet by Ford Madox Brown (1821–1893) (John 13:1–17) This painting, by one of the English Pre-Raphaelite school of painters, was very popular from its first exhibition onwards. The artist shows Peter allowing Christ to wash his feet, apparently rather against the disciple's better judgment, and perhaps feeling he will be glad when it's all finished. *The Tate Gallery, London.*

that the best foundation is rock. In his book *Peace of Mind in Earthquake Country*, sub-titled 'how to save your home and life' (Chronicle Books, San Francisco, 1974), Peter Yanev devotes a whole chapter to 'The relative hazards of various geologic foundations'. He writes:

During the early morning 1906 San Francisco quake, some people living on top of the famous hills of that city were not even awakened by the enormous tremor, and numerous unreinforced masonry buildings located on these bedrock hills survived the earthquake without significant damage. On the other hand, in homes atop the landfill along the bay and the alluvial soils between the hills of San Francisco, people were thrown out of bed by the shock and found themselves unable to get on their feet during the sixty seconds that the motion lasted. Many of the buildings on these flat, thick-soiled areas totally collapsed. (p. 70).

Here, then, is the same fundamental difference. Apart from the immediate fault zone itself, houses built on solid bedrock are safe; 'the highest earthquake-hazard areas are always the natural alluvial soils and man-made landfills in the valley and near the coast and bays' (p. 71). Even 'structures built on solid rock near the fault or epicenter of an earthquake fare better than more distant buildings on soft soils' (p. 72). There are two reasons, Peter Yanev explains, for the danger of soft soil foundations. The first and obvious one is their instability. 'The shock waves of an earthquake are amplified by...soft...soil, and strong shocks can cause compaction of the clay and settlement of the ground surface' (p. 84).

The second reason is called 'liquefaction'. My friend Bill Godden, who is a Professor of Civil Engineering and a member of the Earthquake Engineering Research Center at the University of California, Berkeley, and who kindly sent me Dr Yanev's chapter from which I have quoted, has given me in a letter the kind of layman's definition of 'liquefaction' which I needed: 'Soil which is stable under normal conditions and apparently quite suitable for a building foundation can suddenly change to "soup" and flow like a liquid when shaken in an earthquake. This effect, called "liquefaction", can cause the most dramatic failures; complete buildings may sink or topple over, and large areas may be subjected to landslides.' Liquefaction, Dr Yanev adds, is due to the vibrations, which cause a rise of the water table and so create 'a quicksand-like effect'. He instances the June 1964 quake in the coastal city of Niigata, Japan, as a dramatic example of soil liquefaction. 'Many tall apartment buildings settled several feet and tilted at such a rakish angle that the occupants made their escape by walking down the walls' (pp. 91–2).

I am not proposing to turn the parable of Jesus into an allegory and attempt to find in the spiritual life a parallel to liquefaction. My only purpose in quoting from Dr Yanev and Dr Godden is to indicate that contemporary seismological studies confirm Christ's emphasis on the importance of a solid bedrock foundation.

What, then, did Jesus mean? What are the alternative foundations for life? He was quite explicit. The wise person who builds the house of his life on rock is one who 'hears these words of mine and puts them into practice', while the fool who chooses sand for his foundation is anybody who 'hears these words of mine and does not put them into practice.' Notice that both 'hear' the teaching of Jesus. The difference between them is not between knowledge and ignorance, but between obedience and disobedience. One of the many evidences for the uniqueness of Jesus as God's eternal Son made man is the unassuming yet confident manner in which he could advance such a tremendous claim. The distinction between wisdom and folly in this life, and between survival and judgment in the next, he dared to say, would depend on whether people had listened to his teaching, and had obeyed or disobeyed it.

Jesus made it very personal. Each individual has to decide on what foundation he is going to build his life. Yet what he taught applies equally to the church. The church too needs a firm foundation. And Jesus has given it one. 'On this rock I will build my church,' he said (Matthew 16:18). All of us know the traditional Roman Catholic understanding of this affirmation, which (I could not help noticing) Pope John Paul I and Pope John Paul II both endorsed in their first homilies. 'We must always keep intact the deposit of faith', said Pope John Paul II in his message to the church and the world on 17 October 1978, 'mindful of the special mandate of Christ who, making Simon the "rock" on which he built the church, gave him the keys of the kingdom of heaven'. There is still, therefore, he went on, a distinctively 'Petrine ministry' entrusted to Peter's 'legitimate successor'. Now I am not wishing to write a controversial book. Yet in a chapter on foundations I cannot ignore this question. I will content myself with only two points, the first patristic and the second apostolic.

We need to remember that there was no consensus among the early church fathers about the interpretation of Matthew 16:18. Archbishop Kenrick of St Louis, USA, brought a speech to the first Vatican Council in 1870, which was not delivered but later published. In it he summarized the five patristic interpretations. Seventeen fathers understood the rock to be Peter, eight the apostles, forty-four (including Origen and Chrysostom) Peter's confession of faith in Christ, sixteen (including Augustine and Jerome and later Pope Gregory the Great) Jesus Christ himself, and a few the faithful in general. He concluded: 'If we are bound to follow the majority of the fathers in this thing, then we are bound to hold for certain that by the "rock" should be understood the faith professed by Peter, not Peter professing the faith' (Quoted by W. H. Griffith Thomas in

The Principles of Theology, Longmans Green, 1930, pp. 470–1).

This brings me to the apostolic point. The apostle Paul writes that the church is 'built on the foundation of the apostles and prophets, with Christ Jesus himself as the chief corner-stone' (Ephesians 2:20), while the apostle Peter himself, quoting a catena of three Old Testament texts about rocks and stones, does not apply these to himself but to Christ. Jesus Christ is the 'chosen and precious cornerstone' of Isaiah 28 and 'the capstone' of Psalm 118, as well as the 'stone that causes men to stumble' of Isaiah 8 (1 Peter 2:4–8). We should not, then, be ashamed to sing:

> The church's one foundation
> Is Jesus Christ her Lord.

Nor should we be afraid to teach this truth. It is the point Paul makes when writing to the Corinthians. All Christian teachers are builders, he says, while each comes on the scene at a different stage of the building. To Paul himself had been given the privilege of founding the church in Corinth. He is therefore the 'expert builder', who 'laid a foundation'. What foundation did he lay? The only one there is. 'For no one can lay any foundation other than the one already laid, which is Jesus Christ'. After him along came Apollos and others to build on his foundation. They must be careful about the materials they use, he says. 'Wood, hay, straw' – false teachings of every kind – would be burned up; only 'gold, silver, costly stones' – the true teaching of Christ – would survive the final test of fire on the judgment day (1 Corinthians 3:10–15).

'No other foundation,' wrote Paul. 'No other name,' said Peter (Acts 4:12). On that name we rest. On that foundation we build. Only so can we hope to 'build ourselves up on our most holy faith' (Jude 20).

3
In Christ our Life-giver

'I know a man in Christ', Paul wrote to the Corinthians, 'who fourteen years ago was caught up to the third heaven' (2 Corinthians 12:2). The interest of the reader is immediately quickened. What and where is the 'third heaven'? What sort of journey would be involved for one 'caught up to' it? And who was this 'man in Christ', whom Paul claimed to know and who had this most unusual experience? Well, commentators are virtually unanimous in explaining that the apostle was referring to himself. It was he who visited the third heaven. Indeed, the context virtually demands this interpretation, for he had been writing about himself and had just said that he would 'go on to visions and revelations from the Lord' (verse 1). What is of importance to us at the moment is not so much why he resorted to this roundabout way of alluding to himself, but that having decided to do so he chose this self-description. He was 'a man in Christ', by which he meant quite simply 'a Christian man'. Indeed, if we had been writing the same thing today, we would almost certainly have written 'I know a Christian man who...', which is exactly how the New English Bible does translate it. So then, in New Testament language somebody who is 'in Christ' is a Christian, neither more nor less.

If we need any further evidence to support this statement, we may find it in Romans 16:1–16. Here Paul sends his personal greetings to a long catalogue of twenty-seven members of the Christian community in Rome, mentioning each individual or family by name. Many of them he also describes, and the commonest designation he uses is either 'in Christ Jesus' or 'in Christ' or 'in the Lord'. It is impossible to miss his meaning. For example, he greets Priscilla and Aquila as his 'fellow-workers in Christ Jesus' (verse 3), meaning that they are his Christian colleagues. Later, he sends a greeting to Andronicus and Junias, who, he says, 'were in Christ before I was' (verse 7), which can only mean that they became Christians before he did.

Let me clarify immediately that our third preposition 'in', when used in relation to Christ, is not used spatially. To be 'in' Christ does not mean to be 'inside' Christ, as the family are in the house when they spend an evening together, or as clothes are kept in a cupboard or tools in a box. No, to be 'in' Christ is not to be located inside him or to be locked up in him for safety, but rather to be united to him in a very close personal relationship. Jesus himself put this beyond dispute by his allegory of the vine and the branches. 'Remain in me, and I will remain in you,' he said to the twelve. 'No branch can bear fruit by itself; it must remain in the vine. Neither can you bear fruit unless you remain in me. I am the vine; you are the branches. If a man remain in me, and I in him, he will bear much fruit; apart from me you can do nothing' (John 15:4,5). It is evident from this metaphor that to be and to remain 'in Christ' was to enjoy a living and growing relationship with him. The Good News Bible is quite correct to render the words 'in Christ' by the expression 'in union with Christ'.

The apostle Paul developed two models of this union with Christ. The first is his picture of the church as a living organism, the body of Christ, with each Christian a member of his body. 'Now you are the body of Christ, and each one of you is a part of it', he wrote (1 Corinthians 12:27). Again, 'just as each of us has one body with many members, and these members do not all have the same function, so in Christ we who are many form one body and each member belongs to all the others' (Romans 12:4, 5). Thus 'in Christ', by virtue of our relationship to him, we are also related to one another. Paul's other metaphor is even bolder. Referring to the Genesis statement that husband and wife in marriage become 'one flesh', he writes: 'But he who unites himself with the Lord is one with him in spirit' (1 Corinthians 6:17). This speaks of a deep personal intimacy of love between Christ and the Christian.

For perhaps the most striking of all images we return to the teaching of Jesus. In his long prayer recorded in John 17 he goes so far as to pray 'that all of them may be one, Father, just as you are in me and I am in you. May they also be in us...' (verse 21). This is a request that we may be as personally related to the Father and the Son ('in us') as they are to each other. The implications of this petition are staggering. Jesus envisages that the loving relationship which binds the Father and the Son together in the mystery of the eternal Trinity may be reflected in our own loving relationship with God and thereby in our relations with each other (verse 23).

These different models all portray the same truth. As a branch is united to the tree, as a limb is united to the body, as husband and wife are united to one another, as the Father and the Son are united in the Trinity, so the Christian is united to Jesus Christ. The relationship which is thus depicted is something much more than a formal attachment or nodding acquaintance, something more even than a personal friendship; it is nothing less than a vital, organic, intimate union with Jesus Christ, involving a shared life and love.

Union with Jesus Christ

Having established that to be 'in Christ' is to be personally united to him, there are several important aspects of this union with him which we need to consider at once.

First, union with Christ is indispensable to our Christian identity. That is, nobody is a Christian without it, although to be sure our perceptions and experiences of it may vary. It is an extraordinary fact that people are still debating what it means to be a Christian. That we should be discussing the implications and responsibilities of being a Christian is understandable, but after nearly two millennia it is not a little strange that there should still be any argument about what actually constitutes a Christian. Yet there is. The different ecclesiastical traditions place their emphasis at different points. The Catholic and Orthodox traditions stress baptized membership of the historic church. Protestants emphasize believing response to the Gospel. Pentecostals make much of the power of the Holy Spirit. Others in the liberal tradition see Jesus as essentially the 'man for others', and regard works of Christian compassion, together with the quest for social justice, as characteristic of his authentic followers. I am not suggesting that any of these is mistaken. On the contrary, baptism and church membership, the Word of God and faith, the gift of the Spirit, and good works of love – all these are essential features of a genuinely Christian life. Yet the New Testament definition of a Christian is a person 'in Christ'. It is necessary to insist, therefore, that according to Jesus and his apostles to be a Christian is not just to have been baptized, to belong to the church, to receive Holy Communion, to believe in the doctrines of the creed or to try to follow the standards of the Sermon on the Mount. Baptism and Holy Communion, church membership, creed and conduct are all part and parcel of living as a Christian, but they can form and have sometimes formed an empty casket from which the jewel has disappeared. The jewel is Jesus Christ himself. To be a Christian is primarily to live in union with Jesus Christ, as a result of which baptism, belief and behaviour slot naturally into place.

Henry Scougal, Professor of Divinity at King's College, Aberdeen, who died in 1678 at the early age of twenty-eight, wrote an influential little book called *The Life of God in the Soul of Man*. In it he lamented that so few people of his time seemed to understand what true religion meant. Some think, he wrote, that its essence is 'in orthodox notions and opinions', others in 'external duties' (religious and moral), while still others 'put all religion in the affections, in rapturous heats and ecstatic devotion'. Yet religion's essence is neither intellectual, nor external, nor emotional, but 'quite another thing'. What is this? 'True religion is an union of the soul with God, a real participation of the divine nature, the very image of God drawn upon the soul, or in the Apostle's phrase, *it is Christ formed within us.*' The root of this divine life is faith, and its 'chief branches are love to God, charity to man, purity and humility'. Such outward duties without the divine life, however, no more make a Christian 'than a puppet can be called a man'; they constitute 'a forced and artificial religion' like a forced marriage without love. It was this little book which Charles Wesley lent to George Whitefield in Oxford in 1734, and which was partly instrumental about a year later in bringing him to new birth.

Secondly, union with Christ is central to the New Testament gospel. According to New Testament statisticians, who like to tot up figures and feed concordances into a computer, the expressions 'in Christ', 'in the Lord', and 'in him' occur 164 times in the letters of Paul. I confess I have neither the mind nor the heart to check their figures, although I have no reason to doubt their accuracy. Instead, I call as my witness the late Dr James Stewart, formerly Professor of New Testament Language, Literature and Theology at New College in 1935 on 'the vital elements of St Paul's religion', which he entitled *A Man in Christ.* Here is Dr Stewart's conviction: 'The heart of Paul's religion is union with Christ. This, more than any other conception – more than justification, more than sanctification, more even than reconciliation – is the key which unlocks the secrets of his soul' (Hodder and Stoughton, 1935, latest edition 1972). Similarly, 'in Paul's view everything is gathered up in the one great fact of communion with Christ....Other elements of the Christian experience are not so much isolated events as aspects of the one reality, not parallel lines...but radii of the same circle of which union with Christ is the centre' (p. 147). In thus summing up Paul's teaching, although indeed the emphasis is distinctive, we must be careful not to go back to the old controversy which attempted to drive a wedge between Jesus and Paul, and even spoke of 'Paulinism' as if it were a different religion. No, Paul's stress on union with Christ goes back to the mind and teaching of Jesus himself, and not least to his allegory of the vine and the branches.

Thirdly, union with Christ is a unique emphasis among the world's religions. No other religion offers its adherents a personal union with its founder. The Buddhist does not claim to know the Buddha, nor the Confucianist Confucius, nor the Muslim Mohammed, nor the Marxist Karl Marx. But the Christian does claim – humbly, I hope, but nevertheless confidently – to know Jesus Christ. Members of other faiths look back to their founder as a teacher they revere. Christians also regard Jesus as a teacher and seek to obey his teaching. But to us Jesus is more than a teacher of the ancient past. He is our living Lord and Saviour, whom we know in the closeness of a vital and loving relationship. This distinctive

Christian emphasis Bishop Stephen Neill affirms in the following words: 'Jesus...was a teacher. But Christianity is not the acceptance of certain ideas. It is a personal attitude of trust and devotion to a person. That person is believed to be alive and accessible to all. The nature of the relation of the Christian to him is described in such phrases as "whom not having seen you love", "that Christ may dwell in your hearts by faith", "Christ in you the hope of glory" — phrases which recur in page after page of the New Testament, and make clear that it is this intimate and personal relationship of trust, devotion and communion which is the very heart of the Christian faith' (from *Christian Faith Today* by S. C. Neill, Penguin, 1955, pp.17,18).

Having noted that union with Christ Jesus is essential to the Christian's identity, the New Testament gospel and the uniqueness of Christianity, we are ready to move on to the great blessings which this relationship brings. Here is the eulogy of God with which Paul begins his Ephesian letter: 'Praise be to the God and Father of our Lord Jesus Christ, who has blessed us in the heavenly realms with every spiritual blessing in Christ' (Ephesians 1:3). The apostle blesses God for blessing us with every conceivable blessing. These blessings he calls 'spiritual', and adds that they belong to 'the heavenly realms', a favourite expression in the Ephesian letter, by which he means 'the unseen world of spiritual reality'. The two qualifications 'spiritual' and 'heavenly' are not intended to turn the Christian life into a purely mystical experience, for every reader of Paul knows how practical and down-to-earth his teaching was. Rather he is contrasting the spiritual blessings of being a Christian with the material peace and prosperity which God promised Israel in the Old Testament. He is also hinting that these blessings are available to us only because of Jesus Christ's decisive conquest of the powers of darkness, as a result of which he now reigns supreme 'in the heavenly realms' with all rivals under his feet (see Ephesians 1:19–22, 6:10–12).

Where, then, are these spiritual blessings to be found? They are all 'in Christ'. It is 'in Christ' that God has blessed us with every spiritual blessing. So if we are ourselves 'in Christ', and only if we are 'in Christ', every spiritual blessing from God the Father becomes ours. For in giving Christ to us in the intimacy of a personal union with him, our heavenly Father has given us all the blessings he has to give. In order to understand what these are, we shall stay in Ephesians and look at the three major blessings which are outlined in this letter.

The blessing of a new status

'Status' is an important word in contemporary society. Our self-image seems often to be bound up with our social status. So we all tend to be status-seekers. We enjoy titles and honours, big houses and fast cars, badges and uniforms, and friendships with influential people whose names we like to 'drop' in casual conversation. For these are status symbols. They inflate our ego.

But the Bible offers us another status, spiritual rather than social, godly rather than worldly, far more significant and satisfying, sufficient in itself to build our self-image and give us a true self-worth. It is the status of being a child of God, loved, adopted and accepted by the Lord God himself.

To this status Paul refers in the verses which follow his opening eulogy. In each verse he mentions Jesus Christ and indicates that each blessing he specifies is ours by virtue of our being in Christ. The God who has blessed us in Christ with every spiritual blessing, he goes on, 'chose us *in him* before the creation of the world to be holy and blameless in his sight. In love he predestined us to be adopted as his sons *through Jesus Christ*, in accordance with his pleasure and will, to the praise of his glorious grace, which he has freely given us *in the One he loves. In him* we have redemption through his blood, the forgiveness of sins, in accordance with the riches of God's grace that he lavished on us...' (Ephesians 1:4–8). My italics draw attention to the tell-tale references to Jesus Christ. Each is linked to a distinct blessing. Thus, God chose us *in him* to be holy (4). God adopted us as his sons and daughters *through Jesus Christ* (5). He freely bestowed his grace upon us *in the One he loves* (6). And *in him* he has given us redemption and the forgiveness of our sins (7). The verbs describe the glory of our new status, namely that 'in Christ' God has chosen, adopted, accepted, redeemed and forgiven us.

What greater 'status' can be conceived than to be an accepted, adopted and forgiven child of God? What more do we need than that? As the apostle John blurts out: 'How great is the love the Father has lavished on us, that we should be called children of God! And that is what we are!' (1 John 3:1). This is our high status if we are in Christ. Once we are united to Jesus Christ, God the Father no longer sees us in our sins, for he sees us in Christ. Indeed, he loves us his adopted children as he loves Christ his eternal Son. The New Testament writers repeat many times the joys and privileges of being in Christ. In Christ we are 'justified', or accepted by God (Galatians 2:17; Philippians 3:9). In Christ we are God's children and Abraham's spiritual posterity (Galatians 3:26, 29). In Christ there is no condemnation to fear, for absolutely nothing can separate us from God's love 'in Christ Jesus our Lord'. With these affirmations of no condemnation by God and no separation from God the great eighth chapter of Romans begins and ends (Romans 8:1, 39).

The blessing of a new life

To be in Christ means much more than receiving a new status; it also means receiving a new life. This is an exceedingly important addition if we are to have a balanced understanding of New Testament teaching. Let me give you a recent illustration from the contemporary church in Egypt, which shows the necessity of not separating what God has joined, namely justification and regeneration, the new status and the new life.

My readers will know that approximately 10 per cent of the population of Egypt are Christians, and that the great majority of these belong to the Coptic Orthodox Church. In it during the 1970s there was a remarkable revival of Bible study and renewal of spiritual life. The church's patriarch, Pope Shenouda III, gathered a congregation of between 4,000 and 6,000 every Friday night in St Mark's Cathedral, Cairo. Many were young people. He explained the Bible to them, answered their questions and sought to relate the ancient faith to the contemporary world. But a controversy also developed within the church, at the heart of which was a Coptic priest named Abuna Zacharia Botros. In 1964 Father Zacharia experienced what can only be described as an evangelical conversion, a personal encounter with Jesus Christ. Following this, in his church and church halls in Heliopolis, he attracted between 2,000 and 3,000 people on Thursday nights. With flowing black beard and cassock, silver cross and fat Bible, he cut an imposing figure. He would expound the Scriptures to his eager and attentive people, and emphasize the doctrine of justification (or acceptance before God) by God's grace alone through faith alone. The authorities of the Orthodox Church, however, several times examined him about his theology. And some of his followers were more outspoken than he. When Pope Shenouda published a small book entitled 'Salvation in the Orthodox Understanding', Emad Nazih, a fifth year medical student and member of Father Zacharia's congregation, wrote a counter booklet with the provocative title 'Free Justification and Salvation in the Correct Orthodox Understanding'. He was promptly (in January 1978) excommunicated. Then in mid-May Father Zacharia himself was suspended from his ministry and forbidden to preach. (See Edward E. Plowman's articles in *Christianity Today*, 7 April 1978 'The Priest and the Patriarch' and 21 July 1978 'Egypt: A Crisis in the Coptic Church'.)

What, then, lay at the root of this theological crisis in the Coptic Orthodox Church? It was the doctrine of justification. Between January and March 1978 a series of articles on 'Justification' appeared in the weekly Orthodox paper *Al Kirazah*. Their author argued that after sixteen centuries of agreement in the Church about the meaning of justification the Reformers introduced a 'false and dangerous concept'. They taught that justification is 'a mere verdict of righteousness' without any inward renewal or righteousness of character. That is, when God justifies sinners, he declares them righteous without making them righteous. Luther's mistake (so one article suggested) was to teach that in justification God clothes the sinner with a garment of righteousness, while underneath he remains the same old person in the same old condition. In other words, the Protestant doctrine of 'Justification by Faith' offers a change of status without a change of life or character.

But this is a caricature of Luther and of the classical Protestant doctrine. For it separates what the Reformers refused to separate, namely the new status and the new life, justification and regeneration, the work of Christ and the work of the Holy Spirit. No doubt some Protestants have been guilty of just such a caricature (though not Luther), as if justification meant a free acceptance by God with no ethical consequences. There were those in Paul's day who misunderstood his teaching in precisely this way and spread the false rumour that he encouraged people to 'go on sinning, so that grace may increase'. But Paul indignantly repudiated this slander. 'By no means!' he cried. 'We died to sin; how can we live in it any longer?' And he went on to explain that by faith and baptism we have been united to Christ in his death and resurrection. As a result, we must consider ourselves to be 'dead to sin but alive to God in Christ Jesus' (Romans 6:1–11).

Notice the tell-tale phrase at the end of that verse. Christians are *in Christ Jesus*. It is quite impossible to be justified or accepted by God without being united to Christ. Indeed, it is only 'in Christ' that we are justified (Galatians 2:17). And in Christ we are also new people, living a new life. Paul's strenuous repudiation of works as the basis of justification did not inhibit him from insisting on good works of love as the necessary fruit and evidence of justification. It was the same with Luther. In his *Treatise on Christian Liberty* he wrote 'Good works do not make a good man, but a good man makes the works to be good'. Exactly what the different groups in the Coptic Orthodox Church were teaching I am not sure. But there seems to have been a serious theological misunderstanding between them.

The lesson we can profitably learn is always to keep together the 'new status' and the 'new life' which God gives us. Put differently, we should emphasize the importance of keeping together the two prepositional phrases 'through Christ' and 'in Christ', mediation through him and union with him. Justification is a legal word, the opposite of condemnation, and denotes the action by which God declares a sinner righteous in his sight. But it is not a legal fiction, which leaves the justified sinner unchanged. For God justifies the sinner only if he is 'in Christ', and to be united to Christ is the beginning of a radical change of character and conduct.

Let me bring you back to Ephesians: 'And you also were included in Christ when you heard the word of truth, the gospel of your salvation. Having believed, you were marked in him with a seal, the promised Holy Spirit' (Ephesians 1:13 cf. Galatians 3:14). If we are in Christ, therefore, not only have we received the new status of being God's children which Paul describes in the earlier verses, but we have also received the Holy Spirit. The indwelling of the Holy Spirit is the distinguishing mark with which God seals his people, thus branding them as his own. It is clear, then, that if we are 'in Christ', God both redeems us through his Son and regenerates us through his Spirit. He not only makes us his sons and daughters, but puts within us the Spirit of his Son, who begins to transform us into Christ's image. 'Therefore, if anyone is in Christ, he is a new creation; the old has gone, the new has come' (2 Corinthians 5:17). New status, new life, new creation – we must not separate these blessings. They belong together, and are given to all who are in Christ.

A simple illustration may help. If a vagrant comes to us in dire need, down and out, in rags and tatters, and sick, even starving, it will be good to give him a bath and a change of clothing, but not enough. For he is ill and undernourished. So, in addition, he needs food and hospital treatment. Similarly, we come to Christ down and out, in the rags and tatters of our sin, spiritually sick and starving. In Christ we are at once made welcome and accepted, and given a bath and a change of clothes. God sees us as righteous in Christ. This is our new status. But it is only the beginning. The Good Physician knows we are sick. So he puts his Spirit within us to give us new life and health, and he feeds us with his word until we grow strong and vigorous. There are no half-measures with him.

The blessing of the new community

So far to be 'in Christ' has been seen as the individual Christian's union with him, bringing the great personal blessings of a new status and a new life. We have no reason to be shy about this, for Jesus and his apostles did individualize these things. 'He who abides in me, and I in him, he it is that bears much fruit,' Jesus said (John 15:5). 'If any one is in Christ, he is a new creation,' Paul added (2 Corinthians 5:17). Union with Christ is a personal experience with personal blessings.

Yet equally it has a corporate dimension, and we turn once more to Paul for an exposition of it. 'For as in Adam all die, so in Christ all will be made alive' (1 Corinthians 15:22). In this famous statement the apostle is contrasting two distinct communities. On the one hand, there is fallen humanity, which by union with Adam its founder shares in his death. On the other, there is redeemed humanity, which by union with Christ its founder shares in his life. All of us belong to the old, fallen human race, for all of us are 'in Adam' by birth. In order to belong to the new, redeemed human race, however, we have to be 'in Christ', and this necessitates a new birth. But

once we are united to Christ by faith and new birth, we find ourselves *ipso facto* members of the new humanity or new community which God is creating.

In this new community, Paul declares, the barriers which usually divide human beings from one another have been broken down, especially what he calls 'the dividing wall of hostility' between Jews and Gentiles. For Jesus Christ abolished this by his death. In consequence, Jews and Gentiles are fellow members of God's family and of the body of Christ (Ephesians 2:13–3:6). But that is not all. He has written in an earlier letter: 'There is neither Jew nor Greek, slave nor free, male nor female, for you are all one in Christ Jesus' (Galatians 3:28).

Not that our racial, social and sexual distinctives are literally obliterated. No. Our skin pigmentation does not change. Nor necessarily do our social and cultural practices, or the accent with which we speak. Further, men remain men and women remain women. But now in Christ we are absolutely equal before God, irrespective of our race, rank or sex. We experience a humbling before the Cross. As we see ourselves and each other as equally sinful and equally guilty, we are reduced to the same level and are equally dependent on his grace. So we welcome one another without distinction or discrimination, for in Christ, by virtue of our union with him, we are brothers and sisters in the same family.

That in some parts of the world the church as the new community is more a dream than a reality is a disgrace with which sensitive Christians must never come to terms. All divisive barriers among Christian people – whether racial or social or ecclesiastical – are displeasing to God the one Father, contrary to the purposes of Christ's death and resurrection, hurtful to the Holy Spirit of unity, ruinous to the credibility of the church, and a grave hindrance to its mission in the world. So to be in Christ lays upon us the solemn responsibility to demonstrate the reality of the new community.

If we are in Christ, personally and organically united to him, God blesses us with enormous blessings – a new status (we are put right with him), a new life (we are renewed by the Holy Spirit) and a new community (we are members of God's family).

But how does it happen? We have to come in penitence and faith to Jesus Christ, and commit ourselves to him. It is thus that God unites us to Christ. And this union with him is publicly dramatized in baptism, for to be baptized, Paul wrote, is to be 'baptized into Christ' (Galatians 3:27).

Union with Christ is a living and a growing experience, however. Hence Paul can write both of 'infants in Christ' and of 'adults in Christ' (1 Corinthians 3:1; Colossians 1:28 ['mature in Christ' RSV]). So the question now is: how do we grow in our relationship to Christ? This question brings us back to the words of Jesus:

'Abide in me, and I in you...He who abides in me, and I in him, he it is that bears much fruit' (John 15:4, 5). We notice now that Jesus' allegory of the vine and the branches illustrates a reciprocal relationship between him and his people.

If Christ is to 'remain' or 'abide' in us, we must allow him to do so. Our responsibility here is more passive than active. We have to yield daily, freshly to his control of our lives. We must seek to live moment by moment in total openness to him, so that his life and power flow into us as the sap rises in the tree at spring time.

But if we are to 'remain' or 'abide' in Christ, there are certain active steps that we must take. Let J. C. Ryle, Bishop of Liverpool from 1880 to 1900, express it for us: 'Abide in me. Cling to me. Stick fast to me. Live the life of close and intimate communion with me. Get nearer and nearer to me. Roll every burden on me. Cast your whole weight on me. Never let go your hold on me for a moment' (*Expository Thoughts on the Gospels*, Zondervan Anniversary Edition, undated, vol. IV, pp. 335–6).

The command to 'remain' or 'abide' in Christ portrays a tireless, relentless pursuit of him. It is the spirit of Jacob who cried to the Lord who was wrestling with him 'I will not let you go unless you bless me' (Genesis 32:26). In particular, we need to be diligent in our use of 'the means of grace', to spend time each day seeking Christ through prayer and Bible reading, and to come each Sunday to worship and regularly to the Lord's Table. It is in these ways that we actively pursue Christ and learn to abide in him. The more disciplined we are in our set times of devotion, the more easy it becomes to live the rest of the time 'in Christ', united to him, enjoying his presence, and drawing on his life and power.

4
Under Christ our Lord

Nobody takes kindly to the idea of being 'under' anybody else — with the possible exception of Australians and New Zealanders who declare with relish that they live 'down under'. Words of Latin origin like 'submission', 'subordination', 'subjection', 'subservience' and (worst of all) 'subjugation' all express a degree of domination by another person or institution which we resent. The same is true of their English parallels. An 'underling' is a subordinate of the lowest rank, and an 'underdog' the victim of injustice and exploitation. So who wants to be 'under' Christ? Is not such a position damaging to our human dignity?

It is particularly important for Christians to press this question today, since others are pressing it around us. All inherited authority is suspect, and every claim to authority is scrutinized, and usually resisted. Authority roles — husbands and parents, teachers and employers, politicians and clergy — previously taken for granted are increasingly being challenged. The assumed authority of ancient institutions (family, school, university, church, state) is being repudiated, while in the church Protestants are rejecting the authority of the Bible and Roman Catholics the authority of the Pope. The main reason for this rebellion against established authority is that it is regarded as incompatible with human freedom, and even with our basic humanness. How can a person submit to authority and remain authentically human? That is the question. Now if I had written 'tyranny' instead of 'authority' in my question, the answer would have been obvious. Tyranny excludes freedom, and is therefore fundamentally opposed to authentic humanness. But authority is not identical with tyranny. And Christians want to add that if tyranny destroys freedom, a right authority guarantees it. That is why the same New Testament which emphasizes 'freedom' through Christ (*eleuthēria*) also emphasizes both 'authority' (*exousia*) and 'submission' (*hupotagē*) as entirely consistent with it.

Certainly, the fears and suspicions which many people entertain about a Christian's submission to the authority of Jesus Christ are without foundation. There is absolutely no element of oppression in his lordship, or of humiliation in submitting to it. This is due both to its legitimacy and to its quality. Its legitimacy is grounded in the climax of his earthly career, that is, in his exaltation. Because he humbled himself and became obedient unto death, even death on a cross, 'therefore God exalted him to the highest place and gave him the name that is above every name, that at the name of Jesus every knee should bow, in heaven and on earth and under the earth, and every tongue confess that Jesus Christ is Lord, to the glory of God the Father' (Philippians 2:9–11). The name bestowed on him was not, of course, the name 'Jesus' (for that was given him before his birth) but either the title 'Lord' or, more generally, the rank and honour beyond all others. Once this objective truth of the God-given supremacy of Jesus has been acknowledged, it is right – both for him and for us – that we bow down before him.

Similarly, Paul writes in Ephesians of God's 'incomparably great power' which he 'exerted in Christ when he raised him from the dead and seated him at his right hand in the heavenly realms, far above all rule and authority, power and dominion, and every title that can be given, not only in the present age but also in the one to come. And God placed all things under his feet and appointed him to be head over everything for the church, which is his body, the fulness of him who fills everything in every way' (Ephesians 1:19–23). Here too the historical events of the resurrection and ascension of Jesus are seen in terms of his supreme exaltation, his enthronement in and over the universe. And the words 'above' and 'under' are used to express it. He has been promoted 'far above' all other authority, so that all things have been placed 'under' his feet. These facts are due to the activity of God, and are part of the givenness of reality. The church does not discover its identity by rebelling against this reality, but by joyfully acknowledging it. Christ is the head; the church is his body, his fulness.

If the legitimacy of Christ's authority is not in doubt, nor is its quality. He is 'over' us as lord, and we are 'under' him as servants. But this relationship of submission to Christ, far from crushing our personalities, enables them to develop. Just as children grow most naturally into maturity within the loving discipline of a secure and happy home, so Christians grow into maturity in Christ under his loving authority. To lose ourselves in the service of Christ is to find ourselves. His lordship in our lives spells not frustration but fulfilment and freedom. Such is the Christian conviction which in this chapter we are going to elaborate.

There can be no better place to begin than with the words of the Lord Jesus himself:

Christ at Emmaus by Rembrandt van Rijn (1606–1669) (Luke 24: 30–31) This is probably Rembrandt's most dramatic painting in light and shade, and is unusual in that the artist has lit the main figure, the risen Christ, from behind. *By permission of Musée Jacquemart-André, Paris.*

Take my yoke upon you and learn from me, for I am gentle and humble in heart, and you will find rest for your souls. For my yoke is easy and my burden is light. (Matthew 11:29,30)

Now a 'yoke' was a horizontal wooden frame laid on the necks of oxen. It still is in the rural areas of some developing countries. I have myself been fascinated to watch oxen yoked to carts in Latin American villages, and buffaloes yoked to the plough in Asian paddy fields. Such sights were very familiar to the inhabitants of ancient Palestine. It was natural, therefore, for the biblical writers to use the yoke as a symbol of authority, especially of an oppressive authority. For Israel to surrender to the Babylonian Empire was to 'bow its neck under the yoke of the king of Babylon' (Jeremiah 27:1–15, cf. Nahum 1:13). Slavery was also a yoke, and to 'untie the cords of the yoke' meant to 'set the oppressed free' (1 Timothy 6:1; Isaiah 58:6). The authority symbolized by a yoke was not always tyrannical, however. Different kinds of yoke portrayed different kinds of authority. Whereas an 'iron' yoke spoke of harsh cruelty (1 Timothy 6:1; Isaiah 58:6), Jesus called his yoke 'easy'.

The picture Jesus paints is clear. He likens himself to a farmer, and us to oxen in his service. He places upon us his yoke. Rather, and more accurately, he invites us to take his yoke upon us, in other words, to submit voluntarily to his authority. And he encourages us to do so by reminding us that he is gentle and by assuring us that his yoke is easy and his burden light. We need, then, to explore what it means to be 'under Christ', that is, under his easy yoke. Two spheres are particularly included.

Our minds under the yoke of Christ

First, Jesus expected his followers to put their minds under his yoke. At least, this is how his Jewish hearers will immediately have understood him. For the Rabbis regularly referred to 'the yoke of Torah', 'the yoke of the law'. It was, moreover, a heavy yoke hard to be borne. Not that God's moral law was in itself oppressive. On the contrary, in itself 'the law is holy', 'the commandment is holy, righteous and good', and 'his commands are not burdensome' (Romans 7:12; 1 John 5:3). But the law became a burden to those who tried to keep it either in their own strength, or in order to win salvation by their obedience, or both. In addition, 'the scribes and Pharisees' (whom we meet so often in the Gospels) had turned God's law into a heavy burden by their elaborate interpretations. What God intended as a lamp to our feet and a light to our path (Psalm 119:105) had become a morass of minute rules and regulations. So, in place of the oppressive 'traditions of the elders' – an iron yoke if ever there was one – Jesus offered the easy yoke of his own instruction.

Notice our Lord's explanatory change of metaphor. *Take my yoke upon you, and learn from me*, he said. The farmer with his oxen has become the teacher with his pupils. For Jesus Christ has founded a school, a truly 'open university', in which he himself is the teacher and all his followers are invited to enrol as students. This invitation immediately follows his other and better known invitation, addressed to all 'who are weary and burdened', that is, those who are weighed down with their sin and guilt. They are bidden to come to him for rest. For he will forgive their sins and expunge their guilt, thus easing their yoke and lifting their burden. Now, however, Jesus casts himself in another role. He is not only the Saviour who lifts burdens but the Teacher who imposes them. The only difference is that, whereas our burden is heavy and our yoke uncomfortable, his yoke is easy and his burden light.

The earliest followers of Jesus were quite clear about this. They delighted to call themselves his 'disciples', his 'servants', even his 'slaves'. Humbly and gladly they submitted to his teaching authority. This means that their understanding of truth was shaped by the teaching of Jesus. Having imbibed the traditions of Judaism with their mother's milk, and having been brought up at the feet of contemporary Jewish rabbis, they now had to change their minds about many things under the tutelage of their new teacher. Of course it was a gradual process which, when his earthly presence was withdrawn, had only begun. He then continued their training through the ministry of his Holy Spirit. He himself explained these two stages of their education in this way: 'All this I have spoken while still with you...I have much more to say to you, more than you can now bear. But when he, the Spirit of truth, comes, he will guide you into all truth...he will bring glory to me....' (John 14:25, 16:12–14). Step by step, then, their understanding matured, of God and man, history and eternity, sin and salvation, creation and redemption, faith, love, righteousness and hope, Holy Scripture and Holy Spirit, life and death and final glory. In these and other doctrines they had to choose between current Jewish or secular opinion and the wisdom of Jesus Christ. For these were in conflict with one another. But the apostles were determined to bring their minds and the minds of their hearers under the authority of Christ. As Paul put it later, 'we demolish arguments and every pretension that sets itself up against the knowledge of God, and we take captive every thought to make it obedient to Christ' (2 Corinthians 10:5). It is a fine vision. The multitudinous thoughts of our mind, like the soldiers of a vast army, often rebellious, sometimes mutinous, are conquered by Christ, are taken into captivity by him, and find true freedom in his obedience. To bring our minds under Christ's yoke is not to deny our rationality but to submit to his revelation.

Yet this concept of submitting our mind to the mind of Christ is much neglected in the church today. Too few of us resemble Mary of Bethany. We do not make time as she did to sit at the feet of Jesus and listen to his word. No, life is too busy. Like Martha we are activists. Meditation is foreign to us. We find noise more congenial than silence, feverish activity than quiet contemplation. We need to pray with J. G. Whittier:

> Drop your still dews of quietness,
> till all our strivings cease;
> take from our souls the strain and stress,
> and let our ordered lives confess
>> the beauty of your peace,
>> the beauty of your peace.
>
> Breathe through the heats of our desire
> your coolness and your balm;
> let sense be dumb, let flesh retire,
> speak through the earthquake, wind, and fire,
>> O still small voice of calm,
>> O still small voice of calm!

© in this version *Jubilate Hymns*

But sometimes the 'heats of our desire' suffocate his coolness, and the thunder of our lives drowns his still small voice. Not only is this so, but often we have no wish to bring our minds into submission to Christ. Why should we? We prefer our own opinions. And if they clash with the teaching of Jesus, too bad. Why should we kowtow to him?

It was during the Lambeth Conference of Anglican bishops, on a Sunday in August 1978, that I was preaching in All Souls church on Christ's yoke. The previous day an observer bishop had told me (for I had the privilege of being at the conference as a consultant) that he was 'appalled at the unwillingness of the bishops to submit to the Word of God'. Doubtless this was a generalization, as inaccurate as generalizations are bound to be, for many bishops were deeply anxious to discern and do God's will. Yet this was his impression, and it had some substance to it. Serious theological discussion was conspicuous by its absence, and Cardinal Hume commented on the Church of England's lack of an agreed authority. I was also myself surprised by the somewhat unfriendly reaction of commentators to Archbishop Coggan's appeal to the bishops in his opening sermon to listen to God. It was regarded by some as a gratuitous rebuke when he said 'we have stopped listening to God'. But is this not in fact true of the church as a whole? He went on to describe his ideal for a bishop as 'one who is open to the wind of the Spirit, warmed by the fire of the Spirit, on the look-out for the surprises of the Spirit'. One would wish to add that the Spirit's wind, fire and surprises are not to be sought apart from Christ or Scripture. For to attempt to separate the Spirit of God from the Word of God (whether incarnate or written) has always been a foolish and dangerous mistake.

There is an urgent need in the church today for more genuinely Christian thinkers, who have not capitulated to the prevailing secularism, that is to say, for more Christians who have put their minds under the yoke of Christ. It was Harry Blamires who popularized the expression 'the Christian mind' in his justly famous book of that title (SPCK, 1963). He wrote: 'The Christian mind has succumbed to the secular drift with a degree of weakness and nervelessness unmatched in Christian history. It is difficult to do justice in words to the complete loss of intellectual morale in the twentieth-century church....There is no longer a Christian mind. There is still, of course, a Christian ethic, a Christian practice, and a Christian spirituality....But as a *thinking* being the modern Christian has succumbed to secularization' (p. 3). He defined a Christian mind as 'a mind trained, informed, equipped to handle data of secular controversy within a framework of reference which is constructed of Christian presuppositions' (p. 43). He then went on to catalogue six of 'the marks of a Christian mind'. They are (1) its supernatural orientation (a recognition that the world is God's, and transient), (2) its awareness of evil (original sin perverting even the noblest things into instruments of 'hungry vanity'), (3) its conception of truth (the givenness of divine revelation, which cannot be compromised), (4) its acceptance of authority (God's revelation requiring from us 'not an egalitarian attachment, but a bending submission', p. 132), (5) its concern for the person (championing human personhood against servitude to the machine) and (6) its sacramental cast (recognizing, for example, that sexual love is 'one of God's most efficient instruments' to open man's heart to reality).

To sum up, a Christian mind is a mind which thinks Christianly about everything. It can do so because it has deeply and thoroughly absorbed the presuppositions of God's revelation written in the Bible and reaching its culmination in Christ. Only then can Christians dare to say with Paul 'we have the mind of Christ' (1 Corinthians 2:16). The Christian mind is the mind of Christ because it has put itself under the yoke of Christ.

Our wills under the yoke of Christ

The yoke of Christ has a moral as well as an intellectual dimension, since his authority extends beyond our thoughts to our deeds. There can be no doubt that Jesus expected his followers not only to believe his teaching but also to obey his commands. We saw this in Chapter 2 when we were thinking of Jesus Christ as the foundation on which we build. The little parables which conclude the Sermon on the Mount indicate that the wise people who build the house of their life on rock are those who listen to Christ's words and obey them, whereas to listen and to disobey is to play the fool and construct our lives on sand. Not only did Jesus expect obedience, but he made obedience the criterion of wisdom and the guarantee of security. He also made it the test of love. 'If you love me, you will obey what I command', he declared. The one follows the other as surely as the morning the night. Therefore, 'whoever has my commands and obeys them, he is the one who loves me' (John 14:15, 21).

Again, however, the word 'obedience' grates on modern ears; it leaves a bad taste in modern mouths. Some insist that the Christian life, being one of freedom, cannot be characterized by obedience, since each excludes the other; they have not learned that Christian freedom is found through obedience. Others pick up Paul's catch-phrase 'not under law' and misapply it. They jump to the conclusion that the category of law is abolished for Christians and that he meant Christians were free from all absolutes except love. They do not seem to have come across Paul's other insistence that Christ died for us in order that we may fulfil the righteousness of the law, and that God put his Spirit within us in order to write his law there (e.g. Romans 8:3,4; 2 Corinthians 3:3,6). Indeed, in the Old Testament prophets there is virtually no distinction between God's two promises to put his Spirit within his people, and to put his law within them (Ezekiel 36:27; Jeremiah 31:33). Christians are 'not under law' for acceptance with God but under grace, and 'not under law' for the attainment of holiness but under the Holy Spirit's power (Romans 6:14; Galatians 5:18). For moral standards and so for pleasing God, however, we must say with Paul 'I am really under Christ's law' (1 Corinthians 9:21, GNB). Indeed, the lordship of Christ means precious little if it does not include the requirement of moral obedience.

But is Christian obedience compatible with Christian freedom? people ask. Some years ago a professing Christian girl who was a member of our congregation in London announced her engagement to a professedly non-Christian man. I felt it my duty to ask her if she knew the New Testament's high view of marriage as a spiritual as well as a physical union, because of which it teaches that Christians should marry only 'in the Lord' and should not be 'unequally yoked' with unbelievers (2 Corinthians 6:14–16, RSV). She said she did. How then, I continued, did she feel able to disregard it? 'Because I must be free to choose,' she replied. 'If Christ tells me what to do, if the issue is settled before I begin, I would not be free. And I must be free.' I could only reply that the true freedom of a Christian is freedom to obey Christ, not to disobey him.

It is important for us Christian people to recover this neglected aspect to our discipleship, obedience. Nowadays we all have many moral decisions to make – for example in the spheres of business ethics, sexual practices, divorce and remarriage, the life and death issues of abortion and euthanasia. I am not claiming that Jesus

Christ offers pat answers to complex questions or slick solutions to intricate problems. Nor should we seek them. He wants us to grow into maturity by developing a Christian mind and using it. But there are some moral absolutes and more moral principles in the teaching of Scripture, which we need to hold fast. The Christian way of righteousness, humility and love is clearly enunciated in the Sermon on the Mount and in the ethical parts of the apostles' letters, and beautifully exhibited in the fourfold portrait which the evangelists paint of Jesus himself. We have not been left to grope in moral darkness.

The issue is this: what guides us in our moral decision making? Will a young couple live together before they marry? Will a woman with an unwanted pregnancy get an abortion? Will a couple seek a divorce? Can I get away with this or that business practice? Does it matter if I feel jealousy for one person and malice towards another? How should I react towards my enemies? How should husbands and wives, parents and children, employers and employees relate to one another? What is involved in Christian citizenship and the quest for social justice? How is a local church supposed to conduct its affairs and build its programme? What is a Christian life-style in a world of hunger? May a Christian be ambitious? What shall I do with my money? Is evangelism a Christian duty laid on all God's people? What is the meaning of Christian mission and what are the consequences of Christian compassion? The list could be lengthened almost indefinitely. In every such question or dilemma, where do we look for guidance? Is it really convention which directs us, whether in the church or in secular society? Are we in the end just worldly Christians who follow the crowd? Or do we make a conscientious attempt – by Bible study, prayer and discussion with other Christians – to discover the mind of Christ, submitting our minds to his teaching and our wills to his commanding?

We have seen that every Christian is a pupil in the school of Jesus Christ. We sit at the feet of our Master. We want to bring our minds and our wills, our beliefs and our standards, under his yoke. In the Upper Room he said to the apostles: 'You call me "Teacher" and "Lord", and rightly so, for that is what I am' (John 13:13). That is, 'Teacher' and 'Lord' were no mere courtesy titles; they bore witness to a reality. Jesus Christ is our Teacher to instruct us and our Lord to command us. All Christian people are under the instruction and the discipline of Jesus Christ. It should be inconceivable for a Christian ever to disagree with, or to disobey, him. Whenever we do, the credibility of our claim to be converted Christians is in doubt. For we are not truly converted if we are not intellectually and morally converted, and we are not intellectually and morally converted if we have not subjected our minds and our wills to the yoke of Jesus Christ.

Thus the Christian is entirely at the disposal of his Lord and Master, to do what he says and go where he sends. When I was an undergraduate at Cambridge University during the war, one of the librarians in our college library was a refugee from the continent. He was extremely polite, almost to the point of being obsequious, but he had not yet mastered the English language. When one of us students entered the library, he would rise from his desk, come to meet us, bow deeply and say: 'Please dispose of me how you wish'. He meant that he wished to be at our disposal, but his words made me imagine myself picking him up and dropping him in the waste paper basket.

The church and freedom

Perhaps my exposition of Christ's yoke has so far been too individualistic. Not that there is any need for me to go back on what I have written. If Thomas could fall down before Jesus confessing 'my Lord and my God!' and Paul could write of 'the surpassing greatness of knowing Christ Jesus my Lord' (John 20:28; Philippians 3:8), we have no reason to be ashamed of using similar language ourselves or of emphasizing the importance of the personal lordship of Jesus in every individual Christian life. Nevertheless, the apostles also write of his lordship over the church as a whole. For 'he is the head of the body, the church', the lord of the new creation as of the old, since it is the Father's will 'that in everything he might have the supremacy' (Colossians 1:18). This universal lordship of Jesus is a reality which now we accept by faith, but one day shall see made manifest. For God's plan for the end, when time merges into eternity again, is 'to bring all things in heaven and on earth together [that is, the whole church and the whole creation, both then completely redeemed] under one head, even Christ' (Ephesians 1:10).

It is in the light of this eschatological vision that the crisis in the contemporary church becomes apparent. If the church is in the end to be united under the headship of Christ, it will not in the meantime be united in any other way. Is the continuing fragmentation of the church due ultimately to this one thing, its failure to 'hold fast to the Head'? (Colossians 2:19, RSV)? No doubt many would dismiss this as a ludicrous over-simplification. But I am not so easily shifted from my ground. The stubborn obstacle to the uniting of churches is either the cherishing of traditions which are not in the Bible (the characteristic of the Roman Catholic church), or the abandoning of doctrines which are (the characteristic of liberal Protestantism). I keep returning to this simple question: is Jesus Christ the Lord of the church, so that it submits to his teaching however unpalatable, or is the church the lord of Jesus Christ so that it manipulates his teaching in order to make it palatable? Will the church listen humbly and obediently to Jesus Christ, or will it behave like the brash adolescent it often seems to be, contradicting its master and putting him right where he has gone wrong? Is the church 'over' or 'under' Christ?

One last point. It is under the yoke of Christ that freedom and fulfilment are to be found. Listen again to his own assertion about this: 'I am gentle and humble in heart...you will find rest for your souls...my yoke is easy and my burden is light' (Matthew 11:29, 30). How is this? Many suppose that if any controls are placed on what we believe or how we behave, we would not be free. How can our minds be free, they ask, if Jesus Christ tells us what to believe? And how can our wills be free if he tells us how to behave? They see Christ's yoke and their freedom as incompatible.

Take the mind first. There is only one authority under which the mind is free, and that is the authority of truth. The mind is not free if it is believing lies. On the contrary, it is in bondage to fantasy and falsehood. It is free only when it is believing the truth, and this is so whether the truth in question is one of science or of Scripture.

Similarly, the only authority under which the will is free is the authority of righteousness. The will is not free if it is disobeying Christ. On the contrary, it is in bondage to self-will and passion. It is free only when it is obeying the righteous standards of Jesus Christ.

If somebody asks why this is so, we can only reply that this is the nature of reality, for God is himself the epitome of truth and goodness, and he has created us in his own image so that we find ourselves, our true selves, only in relation to him. He has made us rational beings, with minds equipped to explore his truth and to find their freedom in believing it. He has made us moral beings, and written his law on our hearts (Romans 2:15). His moral law is not therefore an alien standard, but the law of our human being. There is a fundamental consistency between what God is in his own eternal righteousness and what he has 'written' in terms of moral law both in human hearts and in the Bible. It is because of this correspondence between the Creator and his human creatures, between his truth and our created rationality, between his righteousness and our moral sense, that our minds find their freedom in believing his truth and our wills in obeying his law. That is why Christ's yoke is 'easy'. It fits.

'You will find rest unto your souls,' he said. True rest is found not in discarding Christ's yoke but in submitting to it. 'Under Christ' we are free.

5
With Christ our Secret

'With Christ'. The words immediately remind us of funerals and cemeteries. For one of the most popular gravestone inscriptions is the text 'with Christ which is far better' (Philippians 1:23, AV), sometimes abbreviated to just 'with Christ'. 'Almighty God', went the collect of the old 1662 Burial Service, '*with whom* do live the spirits of them that depart hence in the Lord, and *with whom* the souls of the faithful...are in joy and felicity'. And many times we have sung the quaint but popular hymn of James Montgomery of Sheffield, first published in 1835 and based on a phrase in 1 Thessalonians 4:17:

> 'For ever *with the Lord*!'
>   Amen; so let it be:
> Life from the dead is in that word,
>   'Tis immortality.
> Here in the body pent
>   Absent from him I roam,
> Yet nightly pitch my moving tent
>   A day's march nearer home.
>
> So when my latest breath
>   Shall rend the veil in twain,
> By death I shall escape from death,
>   And life eternal gain.
> Knowing as I am known,
>   How shall I love that word,
> And oft repeat before the throne,
>   'For ever *with the Lord*!'

Nearly two centuries previously the famous Puritan minister Richard Baxter had written about death in similar terms, though basing his theme on another expression of Paul's recorded in Philippians 1:22,23:

Lord, it belongs not to my care
   Whether I die or live:
To love and serve thee is my share,
   And this thy grace must give.

Christ leads me through no darker rooms
   Than he went through before;
He that unto God's kingdom comes
   Must enter by this door.

My knowledge of that life is small,
   The eye of faith is dim;
But 'tis enough that Christ knows all,
   And I shall be *with him*.

If the immediate reaction which the words 'with Christ' trigger off in our minds is to think of heaven, we can readily justify this from the New Testament. Our Lord Jesus himself prayed: 'Father, I want those you have given me to be *with me* where I am, and to see my glory...' (John 17:24), just as he had previously promised the apostles in the upper room: 'Do not let your hearts be troubled....In my Father's house are many rooms....I am going there to prepare a place for you...I will come back and take you to be *with me* that you also may be where I am' (John 14:1–3). Then, as he was dying on the Cross, he said to the so-called penitent thief, who was dying at his side, 'I tell you the truth, today you will be *with me* in paradise' (Luke 23:43).

These prayers and promises evidently lodged themselves firmly in the memory of the early church, for they are repeatedly echoed in the apostles' letters, especially Paul's. In First Thessalonians, one of his earliest epistles, which is filled with the expectation of the Lord's return, he tells his readers that the Christian dead will rise first, that Christian survivors will be 'caught up together with them in the clouds to meet the Lord in the air', and that following this glorious double reunion 'we will be *with the Lord* for ever' (1 Thessalonians 4:15–18, cf. 2 Corinthians 4:14). Similarly, in the next chapter he declares that 'our Lord Jesus Christ...died for us so that, whether we are awake or asleep [i.e., whether we are alive when he comes or have died beforehand] we may live together *with him*' (1 Thessalonians 5:9,10).

So the bliss of heaven, according to the vision which is given us in the New Testament, is concentrated in this one prospect, that we shall be 'with Christ'. The words indicate an intimacy of personal communion with him which is far beyond our present understanding and experience. Indeed, in comparison with the immediacy of his presence which we shall enjoy then, his presence with and among his people now is more like an absence. So at least Paul dares to say, when explaining the ground of his courage in the midst of physical infirmity. It is this: 'we know that as long as we are at home in the body we are away from the Lord. We live by faith, not by sight. We are confident....and would prefer to be away from the body and at home with the Lord' (2 Corinthians 5:6–8). It is an extraordinary way of characterizing the difference between this life and the next. Now, in this present bodily existence, those for whom life means Christ and who claim that nothing can compare with the 'overwhelming gain' of knowing him (Philippians 1:21, 3:8, JBP), can yet describe themselves as 'absent from the Lord' (AV). The verb Paul uses means to leave one's country, to take a long journey or to travel abroad. So in this life we are foreigners; only in the next shall we be truly 'at home' for only then we shall be 'with the Lord'.

Every Christian understands these statements and wants to endorse what Paul wrote. To live in God's world in the unseen company of God's Christ is indeed wonderful. Yet we look forward eagerly to something far more wonderful still. One day our faith-apprehension of Jesus Christ will be replaced by sight. On that day we shall see him whom we love, and in whom, though now we do not see him, we believe and so 'rejoice with unutterable and exalted joy' (1 Peter 1:8, RSV). On that day too we shall be 'with him' in a closeness of relationship which will be uninhibited by the barriers of sin and sense. The mists will have cleared, the times of doubt and darkness will be over, and we shall be satisfied with his presence, in which there are 'fulness of joy' and 'pleasures for evermore' (Psalm 16:11, RSV).

Living with Christ now

But not yet! We cannot tamper with God's clock. We have to be content to wait for his time. And meanwhile we are to pursue all the more conscientiously our duties on earth. Was it not a reluctance to do this on the part of the Gadarene demoniac which called forth such stern words from Jesus? This man, formerly naked, demented and uncontrollable but now 'dressed and in his right mind', begged Jesus that he might 'go *with him*'. It was an understandable appeal. He had been made whole. Jesus had transformed him into a new person. Naturally, he wanted to enjoy an uninterrupted, undistracted fellowship with his deliverer. He would certainly not return to the tombs or the mountains in which he had previously roamed, tormenting himself. Nor had he any particular wish to go to the nearby village in which presumably he had been born and brought up. No, he wanted to stay with Jesus. Who can blame him? But Jesus refused and said to him, 'Go home to your family and tell them how much the Lord has done for you, and how he has had mercy on you' (see Mark 5:1–20). He had responsibilities of witness and service which he must not shirk.

That man was the forerunner of millions of other followers of Jesus – pietistic, escapist Christians – who are anxious to be 'with

Jesus' in the sense of opting out of the world. They want to telescope the stages of salvation and jump straight into heaven. It is understandable, but it is also reprehensible. We have to learn to be 'with Christ' now, by faith and not by sight, in the rough and tumble of earthly duty, before we are taken to be 'with Christ' in the everlasting peace of his heaven.

It seems that there were hotheads in the church at Corinth who thought that their life in Christ was so radically new that it released them from all their pre-conversion ties, including their marriage vows, their racial inheritance and their social position. To be sure, Christ has abolished all barriers to fellowship, and 'there is neither Jew nor Greek, slave nor free, male nor female, for you are all one in Christ Jesus' (Galatians 3:28). Yet the abolition of barriers is not an abolition of the realities which distinguish human beings from one another. Certainly, Paul writes, if slaves could obtain their freedom, they should by all means do so. But if not, do you know what his instruction was? It was this: 'in whatever state each was called, there let him remain *with God*' (1 Corinthians 7:24, RSV). Christian conversion does not necessarily change our actual social situation, yet those words 'with God' totally transform every situation because they change our attitude to it. Samuel Rutherford, the seventeenth-century Scottish theologian, imprisoned for his non-conformity, wrote in one of his famous *Letters*: 'Jesus Christ came into my cell last night, and every stone flashed like a ruby.' So too the daughter of General William Booth, founder of the Salvation Army, known to all as 'the Maréchale', during a spell in Neuchâtel prison, Switzerland, wrote the poem:

Best Beloved of my soul
  I am here alone with thee,
And my prison is a heaven
  Since thou sharest it with me.

Wicked men may persecute me
  Banishing to solitude;
They should know my joy is Jesus
  Whom they never understood.

At his voice my gloom disperses
  Heavenly sunshine takes its place;
Bars and bolts cannot withhold him,
  Hide from me his lovely face.

And Peter Yakovlevich Vins wrote to his family from his Russian prison in 1936, asking them to pray that the Lord Jesus would strengthen him to be his faithful witness. 'It is better to be with him in prison,' he added, 'than at liberty without him' (*Three Generations of Suffering*, the autobiography of Georgi Petrovich Vins, Hodder & Stoughton, 1976, p. 41).

These three examples are fulfilments of the risen Lord's promise that wherever we go for him, he will accompany us: 'surely I am with you always, to the very end of the age' (Matthew 28:20).

To sum up, to be 'with Christ' is to be in heaven. But we have no liberty to attempt to gatecrash heaven. For we have responsibilities on earth which we must not evade. At the same time, it is possible to fulfil these 'with Christ', and in so doing to have a foretaste of heaven on earth.

Sundar Singh was born into an Indian Sikh family and converted to Jesus Christ by a vision when he was a boy of fifteen. He immediately told his family. 'Some said I was mad', he wrote later, 'some that I had dreamed; but, when they saw that I was not to be turned, they began to persecute me. But the persecution was nothing compared with that miserable unrest I had had when I was without Christ; and it was not difficult for me to endure the troubles and persecution which now began...' (*With and Without Christ* by Sadhu Sundar Singh, Cassell 1929, p. 102). Soon afterwards Sundar Singh left home and became an itinerant sadhu. In 1929 a book of his was published with the intriguing title *With and Without Christ*, whose purpose was to 'illustrate the difference in lives lived with Christ and without Christ'. Chapter 1 is entitled 'Non-Christians without Christ', and Chapter 2 'Non-Christians with Christ', referring to people who, though unbaptized, 'secretly believe in Christ as their Saviour' (p. 23). In Chapter 3, headed 'Christians without Christ' the Sadhu writes: 'I know there are many who call themselves Christians without having had any kind of experience of Christ. I call them "Christians-without-Christ"....They are like shells without kernels, and bodies without souls' (p. 52). Chapter 4 is called 'Christians with Christ', and is followed by two final chapters which describe his conversion and Christian experience. Sadhu Sundar Singh concludes the book with these sentences: 'without Christ I was like a fish out of water, or like a bird in the water. With Christ I am in the ocean of Love, and while in the world, am in heaven (Ephesians 2:5,6). For all this, to him be praise and glory and thanksgiving for ever.'

United with Christ

I come now to the fullest exposition in the New Testament of what it means to be 'with Christ'. The reader will observe that the same words 'with Christ' or 'with him' occur no fewer than four times within the compass of these few verses:

[20]*Since you died* with Christ *to the basic principles of this world, why, as though you still belonged to it, do you submit to its rules?...* [1]*Since, then, you have been raised* with Christ*, set your hearts on things above, where Christ is seated at the right hand of God.* [2]*Set your minds on things above, not on earthly things.* [3]*For you died, and your life is now hidden* with Christ *in God.* [4]*When Christ, who is your life, appears, then you also will appear* with him *in glory.* (Colossians 2:20 and 3:1–4)

It will be seen from this passage that Paul's concept of being 'with Christ' is something much more than enjoying his friendship, as in the popular chorus 'he walks with me and talks with me along life's narrow way'. It *is* that, for God has called us 'into fellowship with his Son Jesus Christ our Lord' (1 Corinthians 1:9), and we have no reason to be ashamed of the claim to know Jesus Christ as our friend. Did he not use this very word of his apostles, saying 'I have called you friends' (John 15:15)? Nevertheless, to be 'with Christ' is more than to enjoy his companionship. It is rather to share in the four major events of his whole saving career – his death, resurrection, ascension and return – in such a way that we have experienced the first three, and will one day experience the fourth, 'with him'.

First, 'we died with Christ'. To those who hear this assertion for the first time, it sounds (and indeed is) quite fantastic. 'I have been crucified with Christ', Paul wrote, and again 'I have been crucified to the world' (Galatians 2:20; 6:14). And what he writes there of himself, he writes also of all believing and baptized Christians: 'don't you know that all of us who were baptized into Christ Jesus were baptized into his death?' (Romans 6:3). Thus Jesus Christ did not die alone. On the contrary, all his people who have been united to him by faith (inwardly) and by baptism (outwardly) have shared in his death and died with him.

What can this mean? Well, there is no more dramatic way of describing the end of something than by referring to its 'death'. We therefore speak of the death of a wish, a hope, a dream, or the death of a friendship or of a marriage. There is a finality about death; death is the end. So when Paul wants to emphasize that our old pre-Christian life has come to an end, he says that we 'died' to it. Our former life was one of bondage to sin, self, fear and guilt, and to the unseen powers of evil which, because of our estrangement from God, had enslaved us. Did we not sometimes sigh in those days: 'if only I could be liberated from my guilt, from the judgment of God upon my sins, and from the powers of evil which have control over me'? I did. Then I learned that the only way to be set free from sin was for its just penalty to be borne, and that God had done this himself in and through Jesus Christ who died for our sins on the Cross. Next I learned that if we become personally united to Jesus Christ by faith, we die with him, his death becomes our death, so that the penalty is paid, the debt is settled, and we are set free from the bondage of the old life.

Secondly, 'we have been raised with Christ'. Not only have we died to the old life, but we have risen to a new one. Not only has the old life of sin, guilt and bondage come to an end, but the new life of forgiveness, power and freedom has begun. For we are 'with Christ' in his resurrection as well as in his death, so that now our great desire is to 'know Christ and the power of his resurrection' (Philippians 3:10) more and more. The bodily resurrection of Jesus, by which the natural process of decay was not merely arrested but transcended, is presented in the New Testament as the supreme historical demonstration of the power of God. It is linked with the creation of the universe, for it was in fact a new act of creation (cf. Romans 4:17; Ephesians 1:19 ff.). This power of God which was displayed in raising Christ from death has also been displayed in raising us from the death of alienation and bondage, and can be displayed in our lives today by putting evil under our feet (Ephesians 1:19–2:10).

Thirdly, 'our life is hidden with Christ'. Having died and been raised from death, Jesus Christ was then exalted to heaven and enthroned at God's right hand, the position symbolic of his universal authority. This third event in his saving career his people have also shared with him. For having raised us up with Christ, God has 'seated us with him in the heavenly realms', so that our life is now 'hidden with Christ in God' (Ephesians 2:6; Colossians 3:3). Christians have a hidden life. Visibly they live on earth, invisibly in heaven. They are despised, persecuted, battered, even apparently defeated and trodden under foot, yet in reality they are reigning with Christ.

Jesus himself, while on earth, enjoyed a hidden life which people could neither understand nor penetrate. Sometimes his divine glory broke through, as in the miracles, but usually it was veiled. So he was a riddle to everybody, an enigma. 'Is not this the carpenter?' they asked in puzzlement. They could not reconcile his authority of word and deed with his lowly human origins. They could not grasp him or place him. His identity eluded them. Otherwise, if they had understood him, 'they would not have crucified the Lord of glory' (1 Corinthians 2:8).

Today Jesus Christ is even more effectively hidden. He has disappeared from public view. So total is his invisibility, that some do not hesitate to deny his existence. Such is the contemporary hiddenness of Jesus.

His followers also have a hidden life which people cannot fathom. Outwardly we appear to be the same people after Jesus has found and forgiven us as we were before. We have the same passport, nationality, and home. Our parents, husband or wife, children, brothers and sisters, relations and friends have not altered. We have the same coloured skin, hair and eyes. We are still tall or short, skinny or stout, good looking or plain, just as we were before. We even have the same basic temperament. Yet we are new, brand new people! Something has happened inside, which people cannot see. For now we are God's children, accepted and adopted into his family (1 John 3:1,2). Now the Holy Spirit of God dwells within us (Romans 8:9). Now we have received a new life, eternal life (Romans 6:23; 1 John 5:12,13), and this life is 'hidden with Christ'. Of course if it is really there, this new life will show itself in a variety of ways – in a new, humble confidence towards God, in a new serenity in the middle of the storms of adversity, in a new (though still partial) self-control, and in a new love and compassion for people who are deprived or hurting in any way. Yet the life itself, of which these are outward signs, is hidden. We enjoy a hidden life with a hidden Christ. He himself 'is our life' (Colossians 3:10, RSV). If people do not understand us, it is Christ who is our secret.

Fourthly, 'we shall appear with Christ'. One day the Jesus who died, rose and reigns will return. He who is hidden will appear. His second coming, moreover, will be quite different from his first. It will be the same Jesus, the same eternal, incarnate Son, the same unique God-man. But he who came in humility and shame will return in spectacular magnificence. He came incognito, and in consequence was rejected by many. But there will be no doubt about his identify when he comes back; he will be universally recognized and acclaimed.

And when he appears, we shall appear 'with him'. Our secret will be out. Our identity will be disclosed. Our hidden life will be made manifest. We shall be known for who we are, by God's sheer mercy his redeemed children. We shall see and – in some sense beyond our comprehending – share his glory.

So then, the death, resurrection, exaltation and return of Jesus are for Christians much more than historical events. They are personal events, in which we either have participated or do or will participate. Personally united to Jesus Christ, one with him as his people, we have died and been raised with him in the past, our present life is hidden with him, and one day in the future we shall appear with him. This is the primary sense in which the New Testament affirms that Christians are 'with Christ'.

Some practical consequences

The peril of this talk about sharing in Christ's death, resurrection, reign and return is that people suppose it is mythological nonsense, useless for all practical purposes, except perhaps as an excuse to justify Christians' escape from reality. But the apostle Paul did not think so, and nor should we. He expounded his profound theology of Christian experience in order to draw out its implications for everyday living.

In one of his ordination charges entitled 'Sorrow and Joy' the late Michael Ramsey, former Archbishop of Canterbury, spoke of 'rejoicing in the Lord' in these terms: 'To have joy in God means knowing that God is our country, our environment, the air we breathe. "God is the country of the soul", said St Augustine. Living in that country, we do not run away from the griefs of our present environment – indeed we may expect a greater sensitivity to these – but we are in the perspective of God, of heaven, of eternity. I believe that

much of the present obsession of our Church with doubts, uncer-
tainties, negatives, loss of nerve, is due to our failure as a Church to
live with God as the country of the soul. In that country we face
problems with integrity, but we also share in the joy of the saints'
(*A Christian Priest Today* by A. M. Ramsey, SPCK, 1972, pp. 91,92).

First, we have *new ambitions*. It is precisely because we have died
with Christ to the old life and risen to a new life, that we are to 'set
our minds on things above, not on earthly things' (Colossians 3:1,
2). Now this distinction between 'things above' and 'things below',
between 'things in heaven' and 'things on earth' is often misunderstood. Many imagine that Paul is exhorting Christians to neglect
their earthly responsibilities and cultivate a mystical experience. But
these expressions give us no liberty to withdraw from our duties in
home, job or community into a kind of religious vacuum. What are
'the things above'? They are the things 'where Christ is seated at the
right hand of God'. That is, they are the things which are compatible
with his reign of righteousness and peace. What, then, are 'the
things on earth'? They are the things which belong to our old and
self-centred life. We know this because the apostle repeats exactly
the same expression 'on the earth' in Colossians 3:5 (RSV) and
defines these things which we are to renounce as 'sexual immorality,
impurity, lust, evil desires and greed, which is idolatry'. In place of
these we are to 'seek' as the supreme good 'the things above', those
things which please the reigning Christ. We are to 'set our minds' on
them, and pursue them with single-minded determination. Paul's
appeal is very similar to the command of Jesus to 'seek first' God's
kingdom and righteousness (Matthew 6:33). This is to be our
dominant ambition. We are to be preoccupied with God's righteous
rule through Jesus Christ, not in some ethereal sphere but in the concrete realities of our own lives and those of our fellow human
beings.

Secondly, we have *new standards*. Having died and risen with
Christ, it is inconceivable that we should continue to live the same
old life in the same old way. To illustrate his point, Paul singles out
sexual immorality, as we have seen, not because it is the only sin or
the worst sin, nor because Christians have a morbid obsession with
sex, but because immorality is a conspicuous example of 'covetousness, which is idolatry'. It is 'covetous' because it involves the
gratification of self at the expense of others, and 'idolatrous'
because it is an imperious passion which dislodges God from his
throne. Paul does not mince his words. God's wrath will fall on
those who give themselves up to such covetous idolatry. In such
practices, he adds, his readers once lived (Colossians 3:5–7). But
now they have new standards. Instead of covetousness there is self-
control and service, instead of idolatry worship.

Thirdly, we have *new relationships*. It is not only the covetous
idolatry of an immoral life that we are to renounce. We are to 'put

away' (RSV) as dirty rags all the following as well: 'anger, rage, malice, slander and filthy language, together with lying' (Colossians 3:8–9). In their place we are to 'put on' as the bright new clothes of a Christian 'compassion, kindness, humility, gentleness and patience'. We are to forbear and forgive one another, and 'over all these virtues' – as the best and brightest garment of all – to 'put on love, which binds them all together in perfect unity' (Colossians 3:12–14). The reason for this complete change of clothing is plain. It is that the new life to which we have risen with Christ is life in the new community. The old barriers of race and rank have been demolished, for 'here there is no Greek or Jew, circumcised or uncircumcised, barbarian, Scythian, slave or free, but Christ is all, and is in all' (Colossians 3:11).

It is impossible to miss the newness of the new life which Christ brings to all who turn to him. It involves new ambitions, new standards and new relationships. And this newness comes from being 'with Christ'. Paul is laying the foundation of Christian ethics. It is a theological foundation, namely the tremendous truth that Christians are 'with Christ' in his sin-bearing death, powerful resurrection, hidden exaltation and triumphant appearing. If we wish to cultivate new ambitions (seeking Christ's righteous rule), new standards (self-control, service and godliness) and new relationships (humility and love in the new community), then we must remember who we are. We have died with Christ, we have been raised with Christ, our life is hidden with Christ and we shall appear with Christ. The essence of our Christian identity is that we are 'with Christ' at each stage of his saving career. No truth has greater power to transform us. When we grasp it, the radical discontinuity between the past and the present is glaringly evident. We can neither fall back, nor even stand still. We must go forward 'with Christ'.

6
Unto Christ our Goal

The most fascinating biographies and autobiographies are not those which merely tell somebody's story, but those which uncover his or her secret. I do not mean by this that they disclose some confidential information which had not previously been suspected, such as that the hero of the tale was in reality a villain, a secret drinker or drug-taker or philanderer. But rather that they lay bare the direction and driving force of his life, to what he had dedicated his life, and why. The really interesting thing about every person is what makes him 'tick'. For what or for whom is he living? Of course some people have no purpose in life. Either they have sought and failed to find one and therefore lapsed into existential pessimism, or else tempera-mentally they are drifters. They float like plankton on the ocean of life, at the mercy of every wind and tide. Others, far from drifting, seem to be driven, as if by some ruthless demon. An insatiable pas-sion has possessed them, especially the lust for power or prestige. Yet, by contrast, one of the marks of authentically human people is their unselfish pursuit of a noble goal. Those who have developed 'management' skills in business and industry encourage people to apply the same principles to their private life and to set personal goals for themselves. To do so seems to be a condition of mental health. It was while he was a victim of Nazi tyranny in the Auschwitz death-camp that Dr Viktor Frankl (later Professor of Psychiatry and Neurology at Vienna University) began to develop his 'logotherapy'. He noticed that the prisoners most likely to sur-vive were those 'who knew that there was a task waiting for them to fulfil' (*Man's Search for Meaning* by Viktor E. Frankl 1959, Washington Square Press, 1963, p. 165). He quotes Nietzsche's dic-tum that 'he who has a *why* to live for can bear almost any *how*', and adds his own comment that 'the striving to find a meaning in one's life is the primary motivational force in man' (pp. 154 and 164). This 'meaning', he continues, may be a person, a cause, a responsi-bility, a goal, or God.

Yes, God: and more specifically God revealed in Jesus Christ. For the Christian seeks to live his life in all its parts 'unto Christ'. The English preposition renders the simple Greek dative. It indicates that as Christian people we are to set Christ always before us, to keep him constantly in our minds and before our eyes. Our life is to be directed towards him. Our ambition is to please, to serve and to obey him, and our supreme concern is that in all things he may be glorified.

This theme could be elaborated in several ways. The way I have chosen is to show that only when we live 'unto Christ' can we learn to live harmoniously with each other. It is a bold statement, but I believe it to be true. Good relationships with each other depend on a right relationship with Christ.

Our relationships are of fundamental importance. Human life may be said to consist of an intricate web of relationships – in the nuclear family, in the wider circle of relatives, among our neighbours, friends and colleagues. Human maturity is seen in the ability to form stable, loving and responsible relationships. In this sphere probably all of us betray a lingering immaturity, since we all find difficulty in establishing a satisfactory relationship with some people. Although I have no wish to oversimplify, I am convinced that the major secret of harmony in personal relationships – at home and at work, in the church and in the community – is to learn to live 'unto Christ'. When this radical adjustment has taken place, others follow naturally. I propose to illustrate my theme with three examples from the New Testament.

Our relationships in the church

The local church is – or ought to be – a family, a local expression of the worldwide family of God, whose members regard, love and treat one another as brothers and sisters. It is a strange and unhappy fact, however, that many local churches are distinguished less by loving acceptance than by critical rejection. It was so in the first century; it still is today. So we can learn valuable lessons for contemporary church life from the apostle Paul's instructions to the early Christian communities. Consider this passage from his letter to the Romans:

¹Accept him whose faith is weak, without passing judgment on disputable matters. ²One man's faith allows him to eat everything, but another man, whose faith is weak, eats only vegetables. ³The man who eats everything must not look down on him who does not, and the man who does not eat everything must not condemn the man who does, for God has accepted him. ⁴Who are you to judge someone else's servant? To his own master he stands or falls. And he will stand, for the Lord is able to make him stand.

⁵One man considers one day more sacred than another; another man considers every day alike. Each one should be fully convinced in his own mind. ⁶He who regards one day as special, does so to the Lord. He who eats meat, eats to the Lord, for he gives thanks to God; and he who abstains, does so to the Lord and gives thanks to God. ⁷For none of us lives to himself alone and none of us dies to himself alone. ⁸If we live, we live to the Lord; and if we die, we die to the Lord. So, whether we live or die, we belong to the Lord.

⁹For this very reason, Christ died and returned to life so that he might be the Lord of both the dead and the living. ¹⁰You, then, why do you judge your brother? Or why do you look down on your brother? For we will all stand before God's judgment seat.
(Romans 14:1–10)

It is evident that in the first-century Roman church some Christians were 'weak' in faith, while others were 'strong'. That is, some had a strong or well-educated conscience, whereas others had a weak or over-scrupulous conscience. One of the issues between these groups concerned their diet, whether Christians should eat meat, and in particular 'idol-meats' which before being sold by the butcher had been offered in sacrifice to a pagan idol. The 'strong' had no conscientious problems. They knew that in Old Testament days God's people were meat eaters, that Jesus had abolished the dietary laws which distinguished between 'clean' and 'unclean' foods (cf Mark 7:19), and that, since idols had no real existence, food could not be contaminated by being offered to them (cf. 1 Corinthians 8:4–6). The 'weak' were not sure, however. They were probably converts from paganism, who, having renounced idolatry, were determined to have nothing whatever to do with it. Eating idol-meats was for them much too closely associated with their idolatrous past to be tolerable. Indeed, any meat they bought in the market might have been used in idol worship. It was impossible for them to tell. Often the butcher himself did not know. So their conscience bothered them, and the only way they could pacify it and be sure of not consuming idol-meat was to become vegetarians. This was one example of divergent practices between the 'strong' and the 'weak' in Rome. Another concerned the observance of special days.

In themselves these were trivial differences. And there is nothing wrong in having such differences of opinion within the Christian community. We shall certainly not agree about everything until we get to heaven. Meanwhile, we have to learn to be tolerant of each other in the church family. What disturbed the apostle was not the existence of minor differences between Christians, but the attitudes they adopted towards each other on account of their differences. They despised each other and stood in judgment upon each other. So Paul had to write to them: 'The man who eats everything must not look down on him who does not, and the man who does not eat everything must not condemn the man who does' (verse 3).

What is noteworthy is that Paul dealt with this pastoral problem theologically. He did not just appeal to the Christians in Rome to be

nice and kind to one another. Instead, he reminded them of a doctrine which their bad behaviour suggested they had forgotten. It
concerned the lordship of Jesus Christ, namely that he had died and
risen again 'that he might be Lord' and that in consequence 'if we
live, we live to the Lord'. Also if we die, we 'die to the Lord', for after
death we shall be obliged to give an account of ourselves to him. In
life and death, therefore, every Christian is the servant of Jesus
Christ (verses 6–12). This being so, Paul argues, 'who are you to
judge someone else's servant?' (verse 4). We have no business to
despise or judge any servant of Jesus Christ; 'to his own master he
stands or falls' (verse 4).

Mind you, Paul considered the opinions of the 'weak' Christians
to be false. He was not himself a vegetarian. Nor did he see any
reason why he should abstain from idol-meats, since there was only
one God, idols were nothing and the meat was not contaminated by
pagan sacrifice. He could eat without scruple, indeed with
thanksgiving. Nevertheless, as he explains later in the chapter (verses 13–23) and in 1 Corinthians 8, it is right for a 'strong' Christian
voluntarily to refrain from eating in the presence of a 'weak' Christian, lest he leads him to do something against his conscience and so
causes him to sin. Thus Christian love limits Christian liberty. For
Scripture has a high view of the sacredness of conscience. Conscience is not infallible; it needs to be taught. But though consciences
have to be educated, they are never to be violated, even when they
are wrong.

The secret of good relationships in the Christian community,
then, is the recognition that Jesus Christ is Lord and that Christians
live 'unto him'. Many minor issues divide Christians today. I am not
now referring to major issues of either doctrine or ethics in which
Christians should be united because Scripture pronounces plainly
upon them, but to minor issues in which a difference of opinion is
legitimate. How should we dress in church? Should a Christian
touch alcohol? What volume of water is necessary to make a baptism valid? How should we interpret Old Testament prophecies?
Which spiritual gifts are the most important? And many more similar questions could be added. To despise or judge a fellow Christian
on such comparatively trivial matters is not just to get things out of
proportion. Nor is it only an unbrotherly act, a breach of fellowship. It is worse than these things. It is a denial of the lordship of
Jesus Christ. It is a presumptuous attempt to usurp his prerogative.
For who am I that I should cast myself in the role of a fellow Christian's lord and judge? No, we must be willing for Jesus Christ to be
himself, as the Lord and Judge of the whole church. He is not only
my Lord but the Lord of every other believer. I have no liberty,
therefore to interfere in the administration of his rule. My responsibility as a Christian is both to 'live unto the Lord' myself and also
to leave others free to do the same.

Our relationships at work

A second Pauline passage throws much light on the Christian duties of employers and employees:

²²Slaves, obey your earthly masters in everything; and do it, not only when their eye is on you and to win their favour, but with sincerity of heart and reverence for the Lord. ²³Whatever you do, work at it with all your heart, as working for the Lord, not for men, ²⁴since you know that you will receive an inheritance from the Lord as a reward. It is the Lord Christ you are serving. ²⁵Anyone who does wrong will be repaid for his wrong, and there is no favouritism.

¹Masters, provide your slaves with what is right and fair, because you know that you also have a Master in heaven.
(Colossians 3:22–4:1)

There is no justification here for the institution of slavery. The very concept of one human being 'owning' another (however kindly he treats him) is so dehumanizing as to be indefensible. Indeed, the apostle's requirement in 4:1 that slave-owners treat their slaves 'justly and fairly', although it stops short of demanding their release, was at that time a revolutionary call for justice, which led in due course (though much later than it should have done) to the abolition of the whole ghastly system. Meanwhile, Paul gives some radical instruction about how slaves and their masters should treat one another. The principle he elaborates is equally applicable to modern situations of employment. It is that each must discern Christ behind the other. Slaves were to be obedient to their earthly masters, yet 'not with eye-service' (RSV), that is, only when the boss was watching, as if their primary ambition was to please a human being. Instead, they were to work 'with sincerity of heart', conscientiously and wholeheartedly, and with 'reverence for the Lord', out of reverence for Christ and in order to please Christ (verse 22). Whatever their task – exciting or dull, noble or menial, clean or dirty, easy or hard, demanding much skill or only sweat – they were to work at it with all their heart, 'as working for the Lord, not for men' (verse 23), that is to say, as if their service was being given to a divine rather than a human master. For this was the case, as they knew. They were 'serving the Lord Christ' and would receive their reward from him (verse 24). Similarly, masters were to give their slaves just and fair treatment because they must remember that they too had 'a Master in heaven' to whom they were responsible (Colossians 4:1).

Notice that in both cases the teaching is essentially the same. Both slave and slave-owner had the same Master in heaven, were called to serve him, must live unto him, and would one day have to give an account to him. It was knowing this fact of Jesus Christ as their common Lord and Judge which would transform their relationship. The key expressions are parallel:

To slaves: '*Since you know that* you will receive an inheritance from the Lord as a reward' (3:24).

To slave-owners: '*because you know that* you also have a Master in heaven' (4:1).

Each must see Jesus Christ his Lord and Judge standing behind the other, and behave towards the other as he would behave towards Christ. The slave's work would be conscientious and the master's treatment just, because both would have their eyes on Christ.

This simple principle can transform all work and sweeten all relationships. One Christian who learned it in childhood was Samuel Chadwick, who became President of the Methodist Conference in 1918, and from 1912 to 1932 was Principal of Cliff College in Derbyshire. He was converted in 1870 as a boy of ten. This is how it happened. The preacher at his Sunday School anniversary, the Rev. Samuel Coley, told the children a story about John Newton to the effect that if he were a shoeblack he would be the best shiner of boots in the village, because he would clean them for Jesus Christ. This made young Samuel Chadwick sit up and listen, because it was his job at home to clean all his father's footwear. 'I hated to clean boots', he wrote later, 'especially Father's Wellingtons. The Anniversary Sunday was a wet day, and bootcleaning the next morning was at its worst. I began with the Wellingtons, on the principle that the irksome part of a task is best tackled at once. I got through and put them down with a sense of relief. Then as I looked at them, the preacher's words about shining boots as if Jesus Christ were going to wear them challenged me...I wondered if those Wellingtons would look well on the feet of Jesus Christ. For answer I took up the boots and began again. It was a simple thing to do, but I believe...that it was the most important thing I ever did in my life...I got in the habit of doing the simplest duties as unto, and for, Jesus Christ...' (*Samuel Chadwick* by Norman G. Dunning, Hodder and Stoughton, 1933, pp. 30, 31).

Similarly, it is possible to sweep a room as if Jesus Christ were going to pay us a visit that day, and we wanted the place to look spick and span for him. A servant girl, who was once asked how she knew she was a converted Christian, replied: 'Well, you see, I used to sweep the dust under the mat, but now I don't.' It is possible to visit somebody else as if Jesus Christ lived there, to type a letter as if Jesus Christ were going to read it, to serve a customer as if Jesus Christ had come shopping that day, and to nurse a patient as if Jesus Christ were in that hospital bed. It is possible to cook a meal as if we were Martha in the kitchen, and Jesus Christ were going to eat it.

George Herbert, early seventeenth-century poet and pastor, expressed this sentiment in characteristically quaint fashion in his still popular hymn:

Teach me, my God and King,
In all things thee to see;
And what I do in anything
To do it as for thee.

A man that looks on glass
On it may stay his eye,
Or, if he pleaseth, through it pass
And then the heaven espy.

All may of thee partake,
Nothing can be so mean
Which, with this tincture 'for thy sake',
Will not grow bright and clean.

A servant with this clause
Makes drudgery divine;
Who sweeps a room, as for thy laws,
Makes that and the action fine.

This is the famous stone
That turneth all to gold,
For that which God doth touch and own
Cannot for less be told.

Our relationships in the world

Home and work are the two contexts in which most of us spend the majority of our time. Yet God gives us wider responsibilities than those of family and employment. None of us can live as if the wider community had no claim on us. Moreover, in responding to the needy world outside, the same principle which we have been considering can direct and ennoble our service. For an understanding of this we turn to the teaching of Jesus, and in particular to his portrayal of the final judgement under the figure of a separation between sheep and goats:

[31]*When the Son of Man comes in his glory, and all the angels with him, he will sit on his throne in heavenly glory.* [32]*All the nations will be gathered before him, and he will separate the people one from another as a shepherd separates the sheep from the goats.* [33]*He will put the sheep on his right and the goats on his left.*

[34]*Then the King will say to those on his right, 'Come, you who are blessed by my Father; take your inheritance, the kingdom prepared for you since the creation of the world.* [35]*For I was hungry and you gave me something to eat, I was thirsty and you gave me something to drink, I was a stranger and you invited me in,* [36]*I needed clothes*

and you clothed me, I was sick and you looked after me, I was in prison and you came to visit me.'

³⁷Then the righteous will answer him, 'Lord, when did we see you hungry and feed you, or thirsty and give you something to drink? ³⁸When did we see you a stranger and invite you in, or needing clothes and clothe you? ³⁹When did we see you sick or in prison and go to visit you?'

⁴⁰The King will reply, 'I tell you the truth, whatever you did for one of the least of these brothers of mine, you did for me.'

⁴¹Then he will say to those on his left, 'Depart from me, you who are cursed, into the eternal fire prepared for the devil and his angels. ⁴²For I was hungry and you gave me nothing to eat, I was thirsty and you gave me nothing to drink, ⁴³I was a stranger and you did not invite me in, I needed clothes and you did not clothe me, I was sick and in prison and you did not look after me.'

⁴⁴They also will answer, 'Lord, when did we see you hungry or thirsty or a stranger or needing clothes or sick or in prison, and did not help you?'

⁴⁵He will reply, 'I tell you the truth, whatever you did not do for one of the least of these, you did not do for me.'

⁴⁶Then they will go away to eternal punishment, but the righteous to eternal life. (Matthew 25:31–46)

We usually call this 'the parable of the sheep and goats'. It is not a parable, however, but a solemn if pictorial description of the Day of Judgment. The only strictly parabolic element is that the Judge will separate the righteous from the unrighteous 'as a shepherd separates the sheep from the goats' (verse 32).

Jesus tells us that one day he himself ('the Son of Man') will come in his glory, accompanied by his angels. He will take his seat as King and Judge on his glorious throne. Before him all the nations will be gathered. That is, all the people of all the ages of the world's history, whose resurrection is not mentioned but is assumed, will be assembled. Then he will proceed to divide people from one another, as a shepherd with a mixed flock separates sheep from goats, placing the righteous at his right hand and the unrighteous at his left, inviting the righteous to 'come' and inherit the kingdom, and commanding the unrighteous to 'depart' into the eternal fire.

Yet the fundamental teaching of this solemn passage concerns neither the Judge, nor the sentence, but the evidence which the Judge will produce on which to base his sentence. It will be people's attitude to him as revealed in their action (or lack of action) to 'the least' (or humblest) of his 'brothers'. The righteous had fed him when he was hungry and refreshed him when he was thirsty, had welcomed him when a stranger, clothed him when naked and visited him when in hospital or prison, because, he explained, 'whatever you did for one of the least of these brothers of mine, you did it for me'. The unrighteous, on the other hand, also saw Christ hungry and thirsty, a stranger and naked, sick and in prison, but failed to minister to him in his need, because they failed to minister to one of his humblest brothers. They will be judged, he said, not for what they have done but for what they have left undone, for their criminal neglect, their scandalous indifference.

Who, then, are these 'brothers' of Christ? Some have argued that they are the Jews, and that 'the nations' are going to be judged for their treatment of God's people, the Jews. Certainly this was a theme of the Old Testament prophets, and certainly anti-semitism remains a deplorable form of racism. But nations are not entities which have an eternal destiny or can be judged by Christ on the last day; their judgment is within the historical process. What Christ is describing here is the final judgment of individuals, not of ethnic communities.

Others suggest that his 'brothers' are Christians, and that people will be judged according to their attitudes and actions to Christians. Certainly Jesus did designate his followers his 'brothers' (e.g. Matthew 12:46–50; 28:10). Certainly too people's attitude to Christ is often seen in their attitude to Christians, as when Saul of Tarsus, the fanatical persecutor of Christians, heard Jesus ask him 'why are you persecuting me?' But this reference is too narrow for the context, which seems to be alluding to all suffering human beings with whom Jesus lovingly identified himself. This explanation can also claim New Testament support. We are told that 'he had to be made like his brothers in every way', and therefore took 'flesh and blood', becoming a human being (Hebrews 2:14–17). His solidarity with us has gone beyond our human frailty, however; he identifies himself with human suffering and human alienation as well.

How then should we interpret this passage? The whole New Testament teaches this; although we sinners can be 'justified' only by faith in Christ, yet we shall be 'judged' by our works. This is not a contradiction. It is because good works of love are the only available public evidence of our faith. Our faith in Jesus Christ is secret, hidden in our hearts. But if it is genuine, it will manifest itself visibly in good works. As James put it, 'I will show you my faith by what I do....faith without deeds is useless' (James 2:18,20). Since the judgment day will be a public occasion, it will be necessary for public evidence to be produced, namely the outworking of our faith in compassionate action. Jesus himself taught this many times. For example, 'The Son of man is going to come in his Father's glory with his angels, and then he will reward each person according to what he has done' (Matthew 16:27). It is not our salvation, but our judgment, which will be according to our works.

If, then, we are not concerned to feed the hungry, clothe the naked, visit and nurse the sick, and care for refugees and prisoners; if we have no social conscience and no compassion for the deprived and the dispossessed; if we are inactive in face of the acute agonies of the world — then clearly there is no love in our hearts for the needy. But if there is no love for the needy, there is no love for Christ who identifies with the needy; if there is no love for Christ, there is no faith in Christ, since faith without love is spurious; and if there is no faith in Christ, there is no salvation.

Conversely, if we have truly turned to Jesus Christ and put our trust in him for salvation, we shall love him; and if we love him, we shall spontaneously love his 'brothers' — the poor, the hungry, the oppressed — with whom he identifies himself; and if we love them we shall show our love by serving them; and in serving them we shall be serving him.

No more striking example of serving Christ in others is to be found in the world today than Mother Teresa. Born in 1910 in Skopje, Yugoslavia, Agnes Gonxha Bejaxhiu was sure by the age of twelve that she was called to be a nun, and she left for India when she was only seventeen. She first worked as a teacher, than as the Principal, in Loreto Convent School in Calcutta. But on the other side of the convent walls was the squalid slum of Moti Jheel. It deeply disturbed her, and she could not get it out of her mind. So in 1948 she obtained permission to leave the convent in order to give herself to the poorest of the poor. She became an Indian citizen, and in 1950 founded her own Order, the 'Missionaries of Charity'. This 'single frail woman in a white sari', as Desmond Doig, one of her biographers, describes her (*Mother Teresa. Her People and Her Work* by Desmond Doig, Collins, 1976, p. 18; Fount Paperbacks, 1978), this 'enthusiastic well-scrubbed dynamo' (p. 26), began to bring food to the starving, clothes to the destitute, medicines to the sick, compassionate care to leprosy sufferers and refugees, love and education to abandoned children, and dignity and comfort to the dying. Within a quarter of a century she had nearly 1,000 sisters and 185 brothers in her Order, working on all six continents, in Vietnam and Yemen and Jerusalem, among Australian aboriginals, in Africa, Latin America, the United States and Europe.

What is Mother Teresa's secret? On a board in the parlour of the Mother House in Calcutta are inscribed her own words: 'Let each sister see Jesus Christ in the person of the poor; the more repugnant the work or the person, the greater also must be her faith, love and cheerful devotion in ministering to our Lord in this distressing disguise' (p. 113). Desmond Doig describes his first memory of her in Nirmal Hriday, her home for dying destitutes in Kalighat, under the shadow of the Temple of Kali. She was kneeling beside a dying man whom she had just admitted. 'Stripped of his rags, he was one appalling wound alive with maggots'. What did Mother Teresa do? She fell on her knees beside him. Then 'with quiet efficiency she began to clean him as she talked to him caressingly in Bengali'. A young Indian called Christo Das joined her, and then took over. When he had finished he said: 'When I cleanse the wounds of the poor, I am cleansing the wounds of Christ' (pp. 144–5). He had learned this from Mother Teresa, for she has written: 'I see Christ in every person I touch, because he has said "I was hungry, I was thirsty, I was naked, I was sick, I was suffering, I was homeless...." It is as simple as that. Every time I give a piece of bread, I give it to him' (p. 158).

To live as a Christian is to live 'unto Christ'. To seek to do this is right in itself because he is our Lord and we must serve him. It is also a wonderfully integrating principle of conduct. For a right relationship with him leads inevitably into a right relationship with others. In the church family we shall respect, not reject, our fellow Christians, because they are Christ's servants, not ours. In consequence, they are responsible to him not to us, and we are responsible to him not to them. At work we shall be conscientious – whether we are an employer or an employee – because our eyes will be on our heavenly Master. In the suffering world we shall endeavour to love and serve the needy. Because Christ called them his 'brothers' we shall want to give to them the very same care which we would give to him.

The greatest need is to see Christ in every situation and every relationship. We must not put him in a corner or lock him up in a cupboard. We must not attempt to restrict him to Sundays or churches or Bibles or the religious bit of our lives. On the contrary, we must welcome him into, indeed discover him in, every part and every moment of our lives. We need therefore to pray that the Holy Spirit will make Christ real to us, since it is his distinctive ministry to do so, namely to 'glorify' or manifest Christ (John 16:13). Also we must be disciplined in seeking our Lord's face every day and bringing our life and work to him in prayer, for then gradually his presence will pervade the whole of our life, and it will become natural for us to turn to him and talk to him at any time. Then too we will see him in or behind others, and seeing him will treat them as we would treat him. This is what it means to live 'unto Christ'.

7

For Christ our Lover

Christians are said to live 'for Christ'. Although this preposition translates three different Greek words, they all mean the same thing. What is done 'for' Christ is done for his sake or on his behalf. It is thus that we end many of our prayers, beseeching God our heavenly Father to hear and answer us 'for the sake of' his only Son, our Saviour Jesus Christ. The same desire for the honour of Jesus Christ inspires our actions as well as our prayers. George Herbert expressed it in the quaint words I quoted in the last chapter, namely that 'nothing can be so mean which with this tincture "for thy sake" will not grow bright and clean'. Now a 'tincture' according to its Latin origin is a dye or pigment, and so came to be used of any tint or colour. Presumably, then, George Herbert meant that the colour of every action is heightened and brightened if it is done 'for Christ's sake'. He was quite right. For actions are one thing, intentions are another. More often than not, it is the intention behind the action which makes it good or bad, kind or cruel, beautiful or ugly. This is certainly so in the reckoning of God. Jesus taught in the Sermon on the Mount that God looks beyond our words and deeds to our secret thoughts and motives.

Now motivation is an extremely important subject. It is universally recognized that *what* we do matters less than *why* we do it. Industrialists, in consequence, who are concerned to increase productivity, are always trying to discover fresh incentives, either more pay or 'perks', higher bonuses, better conditions, shorter working hours or increased job satisfaction. Detectives investigating a crime ask themselves what conceivable motive the criminal may have had. Psychiatrists also, to whatever school they may belong, probe beneath our conscious actions into our subconscious drives, in order to help us to understand ourselves. Further, although we may define our motives in a variety of ways, Christians cannot help saying that the commonest motivation of all is plain self-interest. For we are fallen human beings, and 'original sin' is an inherited twist of self-centredness. It would be hard to improve on Luther's description of fallen man as *homo in se incurvatus*, 'man curved in on himself'. Human fallenness is human selfishness. Most ambition is selfish ambition. People who 'succeed', because they attain wealth, fame or power, do so mainly because they are driven by an inner urge to self-aggrandisement. This is not pessimism, but the sober realism of Christians who want to look facts in the face.

Yet it would be very cynical to interpret all human achievement as prompted exclusively by self-interest. Because brute self-centredness is frowned upon in most societies, it tends to be sweetened or sublimated in some way. Other and nobler motives refine it. Some of the greatest of human exploits have not been done for the sake of the hero's own reputation, but for the sake of a cause or a person. The sixteenth century European explorers, for example, however misguided they were to rape other countries, sailed the seas in order to acquire territory and treasure for their sovereign. Pierre and Marie Curie, co-discoverers of radium in 1898, and Nobel prize-winners for physics in 1903, persevered against misunderstanding and many setbacks because they were determined to find a remedy for cancer. And what is true of the great discoverers of the world is equally true of ordinary people in everyday life. Children work well at school for the sake of their parents, athletes play hard for the sake of their club or country, and lovers perform best in every sphere when their beloved is watching them.

These are pale reflections of the highest of all motives, however, which is to live and work 'for Christ', for his sake. Christians desire above all else to please him, and to bring honour and glory to his name. Here is how the apostle Paul expresses it:

For Christ's love compels us, because we are convinced that one died for all, and therefore all died. And he died for all, that those who live should no longer live for themselves but for him who died for them and was raised again.
(2 Corinthians 5:14, 15)

Paul begins with the confident affirmation, which should be true of all the followers of Jesus, that 'Christ's love compels us'. The Greek verb (*sunechō*) is used in the Gospels, and specially by Luke, of the crowds thronging Jesus, and of Roman armies surrounding Jerusalem and 'hemming it in on every side'. Luke also uses it in medical contexts of people 'gripped' by fever or dysentery, or by a powerful emotion like fear or distress (Luke 8:45 and 19:43; Luke 4:38 and Acts 28:8; Luke 8:37 and 12:50). In each case there is some strong pressure, physical or psychological, which grasps hold of a person, and controls or compels him. Now the pressure Paul feels upon him is Christ's great love. 'Christ's love compels us,' he says; it 'leaves us no choice' (NEB). The sense in which he feels

hemmed in, almost one might say 'cornered', by Christ's love he goes on to elaborate in a set of four convictions:

First, 'One (Christ) died for all'. All were sinners. All therefore deserved to die, since 'the wages of sin is death' (Romans 6:23). But only one died, died for all, died on their behalf, died (as the context obliges us to add) in their place, instead of them.

Secondly, 'therefore all died'. Not of course that we have all literally shared the same fate, but rather that by being united to Christ we have become identified with him in his death. His death has become our death. It is as if we died with him, thus putting an end to our old life.

Thirdly, 'he was raised again'. His death was followed by his resurrection. Moreover, we were raised with him. For if we are said to have 'died' with him (verse 14), we are also now said to 'live' with him (verse 15).

Fourthly, he died and rose in order 'that those who live should no longer live for themselves but for him who died for them and was raised again.' He died and rose for us that we might live for him.

There is an irresistible logic in the love of Christ. The new life we live today, if we belong to Christ, we owe entirely to his love who gave himself for us on the Cross and then was raised from death. It is 'because we are convinced' (verse 14) of these truths about Christ's death and resurrection that 'Christ's love compels us'. It is inconceivable that we should now live for ourselves. How could we? Since we owe our new life to him, we must inevitably live it for him. The love of Christ hems us in; it leaves us no alternative.

This new life which we are to live for Christ takes many forms. We will consider some of its main aspects.

Christian obedience is for Christ

We have already seen that we are 'under' the authority of Christ as Lord, and are to build our lives 'on' the solid foundation of his teaching. Now we are ready to grasp the rationale of this Christian obedience. It is to be found in the uniqueness of the person who commands it. Christian obedience is 'for' Christ.

Simon Peter gives us a good example from his fishing career. It seems to have been early morning by the lakeside of Galilee. After a fruitless night of fishing, Peter, James and John, who were partners in a fishing business on the lake, were disconsolately washing their nets on the shore. After borrowing and launching Simon's boat, and using it as a pulpit from which to teach the people, Jesus said to Simon: 'Put out into deep water, and let down the nets for a catch.' Simon protested. 'Master, we've worked hard all night and haven't caught anything.' All his fishing expertise, learned from his father and tested by hard experience, rebelled against the suggestion. Jesus was telling him to do something which he knew to be absurd. If his brother Andrew had told him to do it, or James and John his partners, or some other dunderhead, he would have told them to go and get their heads examined. But it was not they who were speaking, it was Jesus. Somehow that made all the difference. In effect, Simon Peter said to Jesus: 'Lord, I wouldn't do it for anybody else. But because it's you who tell me, I will let down the nets'. And we know what happened: such a large catch that the nets nearly broke, a second boat was needed, and both boats almost sank under the weight of fish (Luke 5:1–11).

Christian obedience is unlike every other kind of obedience. It is not the obedience of slaves or soldiers, but essentially the obedience of lovers, who know, trust and love the person who issues the commands. This at least is how John records Jesus as explaining and justifying the obedience for which he asked:

> [15]*If you love me, you will obey what I command...*[21]*Whoever has my commands and obeys them, he is the one who loves me. He who loves me will be loved by my Father, and I too will love him and show myself to him...*[23]*If anyone loves me, he will obey my teaching. My Father will love him, and we will come to him and make our home with him.*
> (John 14:15,21,23)

I confess that these are favourite verses of mine and have often been both an encouragement and a challenge to me. Jesus assumes that his followers will love him, indeed (according to the synoptic evangelists) that we will love him more than our parents, children, spouse, brothers and sisters (Matthew 10:37; Luke 14:26). Knowing full well that the Old Testament command was to love God first and with all our being, Jesus nevertheless expects his disciples to give their supreme love to him. Further, he is clear how he wants us to express our love for him: not primarily by protestations of loyalty, or by singing sentimental 'hymns of personal devotion' (as the old hymnbooks used to call them), but by 'having' his commandments (i.e. searching them out from his teaching and storing them up in our minds) and by 'obeying' them. Moreover, to the disciple who proves his love by obedience, Jesus makes an exceptional promise: 'I will love him and show myself to him' (verse 21). Again, 'My Father will love him, and we will come to him and make our home with him' (verse 23). It would be hard to conceive richer promises than these. Christ promises to his lovers that he and his Father will come and dwell with them, and that he will make himself known to them. The test of love is obedience, and the reward of love a self-manifestation of Jesus Christ.

There are times in every Christian's life when we are sorely tempted to disobey Christ, either because we do not like what he commands, or because we do not understand why he should command it, or because we think we know better, or because the commanded thing is out of fashion. It is at times like these that we need to remember the rationale of obedience. The love of Christ compels us. It has awakened our love for him. 'For his sake', because it is he who commands us, we will gladly and promptly obey.

Christian mission is for Christ

It is necessary now to return in our minds to 2 Corinthians 5 and to the two verses which conclude the chapter:

> ²⁰So we are ambassadors for Christ, God making his appeal through us. We beseech you on behalf of Christ, be reconciled to God. ²¹For our sake he made him to be sin who knew no sin, so that in him we might become the righteousness of God.
> (2 Corinthians 5:20, 21, RSV)

The contrast between these verses is striking. According to verse 21, in one of the most sensational expressions in the whole New Testament, it was 'for our sake' (*huper hēmōn*) that God actually made the sinless Christ to be sin on the Cross, by causing him to bear our sins. According to verse 20 it is 'for Christ's sake' (*huper Christou*) that we are ambassadors and 'for Christ's sake' (the same words are repeated) that we beg people to be reconciled to God. Thus, because Christ acted for our sake we now act for his. The Cross of Christ was undertaken for us; the Christian mission must be undertaken for him. The thought goes back to the teaching of Jesus himself: 'whoever loses his life for my sake and the Gospel's will save it' (Mark 8:35, RSV). Edward H. Bickersteth, Bishop of Exeter from 1885 to 1906, echoed this in his stirring missionary hymn:

> For my sake and the Gospel's go
> And tell redemption's story.
> His heralds answer 'Be it so,
> And thine, Lord, all the glory!'
> They preach his birth, his life, his Cross,
> The love of his atonement,
> For whom they count the world but loss,
> His Easter, his enthronement.

Since the whole concept of evangelism is out of favour in many parts of the church today, and since the great majority of Christians could hardly be described as zealous witnesses to Jesus Christ, it is necessary to pursue the question of missionary motives. Why should we desire to win our relatives and friends for Christ? On what grounds can cross-cultural messengers of the gospel justify their endeavour to convert to Christ the adherents of other religions? The apostles would have answered these questions without difficulty or hesitation. All Christian mission is undertaken 'for the sake of Christ'.

Here is Paul's statement near the beginning of his letter to the

Romans. He had received 'grace and apostleship' from Jesus Christ and 'for his name's sake' he wrote, in order to call the nations to the obedience of faith (Romans 1:5). In similar terms the apostle John described the earliest missionaries. They had gone out, he wrote 'for the sake of the Name' (3 John 7). We are not even told whose name is meant. But there is no need; we know without being told. It is the name that is above every name, the name of Jesus Christ. For the sake of that name Christian missionaries of every generation have left their homes, identified with another culture, risked danger, disease and death. Their primary motivation has always been and still is that the name of Jesus Christ should be given the honour it deserves.

In my reading of missionary biographies I have not come across a better example of this than that of Henry Martyn who in 1805 left England for India, and later moved on to Iran as an ambassador for Jesus Christ. A brilliant Cambridge scholar, he translated the New Testament into both Hindi and Persian, in order to share the good news of Christ with Moslems, who spoke those languages. His Christian devotion was so intense, almost passionate, that any insult to Jesus cut him to the quick. In Shiraz about a year before his untimely death at the age of thirty-one, somebody said in his presence that the crown prince of Persia had killed so many Russian Christians in battle that Christ had taken hold of Mohammed's skirt and begged him to stop. Here was Christ kneeling before Mohammed. It was a bold, even a shocking, statement. 'I was cut to the soul at this blasphemy', Henry Martyn wrote in his journal. 'I could not endure existence if Jesus were not glorified; it would be hell to me, if he were to be always thus dishonoured' (*Henry Martyn: Confessor of the Faith* by Constance E. Padwick, IVP, 1922, new edition 1953, p. 146).

I clearly remember my sense of astonishment and shame when I first read those words. It remains with me to this day, for I have never experienced so complete a personal identification with Christ as to feel insults to Jesus as if they were directed at me. Nevertheless, at least I think I understand what Henry Martyn was describing. I am also sure we need to apply the same principle to ourselves, even if we stay at home and never get within a thousand miles of becoming a cross-cultural missionary. Some of our relatives and friends do not know Jesus Christ. We have colleagues at work to whom he is a stranger. In London where I live there are millions of people who walk down the streets, and jam the tubes and buses in the rush hour, who neither know, nor acknowledge Christ. Instead of honouring his name, they profane it. Instead of exalting it, they trample it under foot. How do we feel about it? Do we care? Are we wounded in spirit, even to the smallest degree, that he is not receiving the glory he deserves? It is this zeal, even 'jealousy', for the honour of Christ's name which is the strongest, the highest, the noblest motive for all Christian mission.

Christian suffering is for Christ

It comes as a novel idea to many that Jesus expected his followers to suffer for him, just as for his sake he expected them to obey and to witness. Yet the fact is irrefutable. Two quotations from Christ's own lips will be enough to demonstrate it, the first being the eighth beatitude in the Sermon on the Mount, and the second belonging to the so-called 'apocalyptic discourse' at the end of his ministry.

> *Blessed are those who are persecuted because of righteousness, for theirs is the kingdom of heaven. Blessed are you when people insult you, persecute you and falsely say all kinds of evil against you because of me. Rejoice and be glad....* (Matthew 5:10–12)
>
> *Then you will be handed over to be persecuted and put to death, and you will be hated by all nations* because of me. (Matthew 24:9)

Jesus' prediction was amply fulfilled. The story is told in the Acts of the Apostles. Peter and John, for example, who were first flogged and then strictly forbidden to speak any more in the name of Jesus, left the meeting of the Jewish Council 'rejoicing because they had been counted worthy of suffering disgrace *for the Name*' (Acts 5:40, 41). The most conspicuous example of suffering for Christ, however, was the apostle Paul. Almost immediately after his conversion Jesus sent him a message via Ananias: 'I will show him how much he must suffer *for my name*'. After the first missionary journey, which took him and Barnabas through Cyprus and Galatia, they were described as 'men who have risked their lives *for the name of our Lord Jesus Christ*' (Acts 9:16; 15:26).

Paul described his own sufferings in similar or identical terms. Here are some examples:

> We are fools *for Christ's sake* (1 Corinthians 4:10, RSV).
>
> We who are alive are always being given over to death *for Jesus' sake* (2 Corinthians 4:11).
>
> *For Christ's sake*....I delight in weaknesses, in insults, in hardships, in persecutions, in difficulties (2 Corinthians 12:10).
>
> I am ready not only to be bound, but also to die in Jerusalem *for the name of the Lord Jesus* (Acts 21:13).

And what Paul experienced himself he expected, at least in some measure, to be the common lot of all Christian believers. Indeed, he links faith in Christ and suffering for Christ as twin gifts of God to his people:

> It has been granted to you *on behalf of* Christ not only to believe on him, but also to suffer *for him*.... (Philippians 1:29,30)

The same two gifts are given together, the believing and the suffering, to many Christians throughout the world today. As we sit in the security and comfort of our Western churches, there are thousands of humble Christian believers – especially in Moslem and

(until recently) in Marxist countries – who are inhibited and persecuted in various ways because of their allegiance to Jesus Christ. I
have a friend who has laboured for many years as a medical missionary in a particular Moslem country. At a time when a local news-
paper was carrying bitter attacks on the Christian faith, he wrote:
'It seems to be our lot as Christians to be misunderstood, criticized
and opposed by the world; and while the poor, the diseased, the
blind and the spiritually hungry come to us in their need, and in their
hundreds, some of the wise, the rich and the self-sufficient spend
their time slandering and opposing us, as they did when the Lord
Jesus lived among them in the flesh....It is the greatest privilege in the
world to be spat upon *for his sake*. Oh that we were more worthy
of it!'

Christians have also been suffering under totalitarian Marxism.
Perhaps the most impressive recent example is that of the Vins family in the Soviet Union. The autobiography of Georgi Petrovich
Vins, General Secretary of the Council of Evangelical Christian-
Baptist Churches, was published in 1976 under the title *Three Generations of Suffering* (Keston Books No. 3, published by Hodder &
Stoughton, 1976). He documents the persecutions endured by his
father Peter Yakovlevich Vins, who, after preaching the gospel in
the thirties in Siberia and the Far East, died in 1943 in a labour
camp; by his mother Lidia who was arrested and tried in 1970 and
1971; and by himself during his imprisonment from 1966 to 1969.
In 1974 he was re-arrested. In April that year his four children
addressed a poignant letter to Mr Kosygin and Mr Podgorny at the
Kremlin, pleading for his release and showing how they too were
now suffering from repressions, as their parents and grandparents
had suffered before them (pp. 211–2). The letter went unheeded. In
January 1975 their father was sentenced to five years' imprisonment, followed by five years' exile. Then his son Peter was also sent
to prison for one year. In April 1979, after having completed his
prison sentence, Georgi Vins was expelled from the Soviet Union,
and continued his work for the Unregistered Baptist Churches from
the United States. More than ten years later, in August 1990, in the
new climate of *glasnost*, Georgi Vins, along with other exiled Rus-
sians such as Alexander Solzhenitsyn, had his Soviet citizenship
restored.

What is it that inspired three generations of the Vins family to
endure such pitiless persecution? Let Georgi Vins reply. Quoting
from Hebrews 11:24–26, in which Moses is described as 'choosing
rather to share ill-treatment with the people of God than to enjoy
the fleeting pleasures of sin', because he 'considered abuse suffered
for Christ greater wealth than the treasures of Egypt', Pastor Vins
wrote: 'these were my father's favourite verses. Like many Russian
Christians of his time, he had a profound understanding of the biblical truth that it is better to suffer with God's people, better to

bear the vilification of Christ, than to have transient sinful enjoyment and earthly treasures' (p. 29). He has carefully preserved a poem which his father sent him from the labour camp for his fourth birthday, 'because it contains the sacred testament of a prisoner-father to his four-year-old son'. Here is one of its verses:

> Now you are forced involuntarily
> To suffer for the name of the Lord,
> But I pray that you may willingly
> Choose the thorny path of Christ.

This, indeed, the Vins family have done, and the whole Christian church honours them for their faithfulness and courage.

The last time actual physical violence was directed against Christians in Britain in any systematic way was probably between 1880 and 1884, soon after the Salvation Army had been so called. Here is Richard Collier's description of the cruel assaults which the Salvationists had to endure:

> *All too conscious that the Army had driven deep salients into the heart of their territory, publicans and brothel-keepers were launching a savage all-out counter-attack....The Army learned the bleak truth of the Spanish proverb: 'he who would be a Christian must expect crucifixion'....In Whitechapel lasses were first roped together like cattle, then pelted with live coals. On dark nights, hooligans used sprinklers to shower the marching troops with tar and burning sulphur....*
>
> *Booth was often in the thick of it. When a kerbside rough spat at him on one Midlands tour, Booth curbed a solicitous aide: 'Don't rub it off – it's a medal!'*
>
> *In one year alone – 1882 – 669 Salvation Army soldiers were knocked down or brutally assaulted. 60 buildings were virtually wrecked by the mob....*
>
> *As Britain's police turned the blindest of eyes, the mobs' audacity grew. 100 young toughs in Oldham, Lancs, who booted the lasses without mercy, were among the first to organise a 'Skeleton Army', but within weeks the sick virus of hatred had infected the nation. When the Skeletons opened subscription-lists, brewers and publicans weighed in generously....They took their name from the skull-and-crossbones banners they adopted, inscribed with strange legends – gorillas, rats, even Satan himself....*
>
> *When Salvationists dedicated their children in the 1880s, they were told: 'You must be willing that the child should spend all its life in the Salvation Army, wherever God should choose to send it, that it should be despised, hated, cursed, beaten, kicked, imprisoned or killed for Christ's sake'.* (The General Next to God by Richard Collier, Collins, 1965, Fontana, 1968, pp. 104–109).

But all that was more than a century ago. Britain today seems to belong to a different world. Now the church is not persecuted so much as ignored. Its revolutionary message has been reduced to a toothless creed for bourgeois suburbanites. Nobody opposes it any longer, because really it neither says nor does anything much to oppose. My own conviction, for what it is worth, is that if we Christians were to compromise less, we would undoubtedly suffer more. If we were to hold fast the old-fashioned gospel of Christ crucified for sinners, and of salvation as an absolutely free and undeserved gift, then the Cross would again become a stumbling block to the proud. If we were to maintain the high moral standards of Jesus – of uncorruptible honesty and integrity, of chastity before marriage and fidelity in it, and of costly, self-sacrificial love – then there would be a public outcry that the church had returned to Puritanism. If we were to dare once more to talk plainly about the alternatives of life and death, salvation and judgment, heaven and hell, then the world would rise up in anger against such 'old-fashioned rubbish'. Physical violence, imprisonment and death may not be the fate of Christians in the West today, but faithfulness to Jesus Christ will without any doubt bring ridicule and ostracism. This should not surprise us, however, for we are followers of the suffering Christ. Nor should it offend us. On the contrary, we should seek his grace to count it a privilege to live, to suffer and to die 'for his sake'.

'Christ's love compels us.' It is from a profound sense of indebtedness to the Christ who has loved us that 'for his sake' we should be prompt to obey, eager to witness, and ready to suffer. To live 'for Christ' is to live always within sight of the Cross. Nobody can teach us this lesson better than Count Zinzendorf. Let me tell you his story. (See also *Zinzendorf, the Ecumenical Pioneer*, 'a study in the Moravian contribution to Christian mission and unity' by A. J. Lewis, SCM, 1962.)

Nikolaus Ludwig von Zinzendorf was born in Dresden in 1700 into the Austrian nobility. After studying law at the University of Wittenberg and then entering the Saxon civil service, he retired at the early age of twenty-seven in order to devote himself to Herrnhut, the Christian community he had started five years previously for religious fugitives from Moravia. Zinzendorf's life was dominated by two major concerns.

The first was worldwide evangelization. While he was still at school, he and five other boys founded what they called 'The Order of the Grain of Mustard Seed', whose object was to carry the gospel to the ends of the earth. Its members wore a ring inscribed with the words (in Greek) 'no one lives to himself'. Soon prominent churchmen and statesmen were included among the members of the Order. In due course missionaries from Herrnhut took the good news to slaves in the West Indies, Eskimos in Greenland, Indians in North America, Hottentots in South Africa and negroes in South America. By 1760, the year of Zinzendorf's death, he had 226 missionaries at work from the Arctic to the Tropics, and from America to Asia. Dr Gustav Warneck commented: 'The Moravian Church had done more for the heathen than all the other Protestant churches put together' (p. 80). Zinzendorf is of particular interest to us in Britain because John Wesley owed his conversion under God to the Moravians, and he derived from them many features of early Methodism like class meetings, love feasts and hymn-singing.

Zinzendorf's second preoccupation was the unity of the church. He did not want Lutherans, Calvinists, Anglicans or others to lose their distinctive emphases, but he longed to see all Christians who had 'experienced the death of Jesus in their hearts' (p. 15) united in a fellowship or commonwealth of churches. Apparently he was the first person to use the Greek word *oikoumenē* to mean 'the worldwide Christian church' (p. 13).

Such, then, was his double commitment: world evangelism and church unity. What was the inspiration for these concerns? They were 'the outgrowth of one supreme devotion: Zinzendorf's simple unquestioning, unyielding and all-embracing devotion to the Lamb of God'. 'I have but one passion,' he declared, ''tis he, 'tis only he' (p. 12). Brought up by his grandmother in the tradition of Bohemian pietism, which had reacted against cold Lutheran orthodoxy, he loved Jesus Christ from his childhood, and determined before he was ten years old to be a preacher of the Gospel. His major emphasis was on *Herzensreligion*, an intense personal heart-devotion to Jesus as the Saviour who had died for him.

If he had a spiritual crisis in his life, it was when he was nineteen. Newly graduated in law, he was sent off (like every eighteenth-century nobleman) to complete his education and become 'a man of the world' by touring European cities, beginning with Paris. 'If the object of my being sent to France is to make me a man of the world,' he wrote, 'I declare that this is money thrown away; for God will in his goodness preserve me in the desire to live only for Jesus Christ'. In Düsseldorf he visited the art gallery and was arrested by a masterly painting of Jesus Christ by Domenico Fetti, the early seventeenth-century Italian artist. It was his *Ecce Homo*, now in Munich, portraying Jesus as Pilate presented him to the crowd after his scourging – clothed in purple, bound with ropes, and crowned with thorns. Zinzendorf stood before it transfixed. The eyes of Christ seemed to penetrate his heart, while the words of Christ written in Latin above and beneath the painting seemed to be addressed directly to him:

> This I did for you;
> What are you doing for me?

'There and then,' writes A. J. Lewis, 'the young Count asked the crucified Christ to draw him into 'the fellowship of his sufferings' and to open up a life of service to him' (pp. 28,29).

It so happens that in All Souls Church in London there hangs on the east wall behind the Communion Table another *Ecce Homo* (see p. 104). Painted by Richard Westall, it was presented to the church at its opening in 1824 by King George IV. It depicts Christ, handcuffed, thorn-crowned and in a purple cloak. Round his head are three hands, the hands of jeering priests and soldiers, who are all looking and pointing at him. Yet what they did in scorn and derision, we seek to do in faith, love and worship. Our whole ministry aims to be a testimony to him. And down the years thousands of worshippers have stood or knelt before this picture, as Zinzendorf did before his, and prayed that, in response to his great love for us, we may live our lives for him.

8
Like Christ our Model

'You became imitators of us and of the Lord' (1 Thessalonians 1:6). 'Follow my example, as I follow the example of Christ' (1 Corinthians 11:1). So wrote the apostle Paul to two early Christian communities. The first text is a statement, the second an exhortation. But both emphasize that beyond the following of the apostles there is to be a following of Christ. This theme has been the more familiar to Christians throughout the world during the last half millenium because of the publication at the beginning of the fifteenth century of Thomas à Kempis' spiritual classic *The Imitation of Christ*. His first chapter is entitled 'On Imitating Christ' and begins: '"He who follows me can never walk in darkness", says the Lord. By these words Christ urges us to mould our lives and characters in the image of his, if we wish to be truly enlightened and freed from all blindness of heart. Let us therefore see that we endeavour beyond all else to meditate on the life of Jesus Christ.'

But how can one imitate Christ? The superficial may suppose it to be easy. But Thomas à Kempis bids us meditate before we attempt to imitate, and he who meditates on that unique life sees a great gulf between him and us, the gulf between perfection and sin. Consider his single-minded devotion to the Father, and to the Father's will, from which nothing would deflect him, though it meant the pain and dereliction of the Cross; then consider our wanderings into the far country, our wilfulness, our feeble and flabby compromises. Or see his strong self-mastery and tender compassion to the needy, which we pervert into hard-heartedness towards the weaknesses of others and softness towards our own. The gulf is wide indeed, even impassable. How can we imitate him?

Besides, he is not only high above us in his attainment, but far away from us as well. We do not see him clearly. First-century Palestine is exceedingly remote from twentieth-century London or New York or Lagos or Tokyo. The mists blur our vision.

Dim tracts of time divide
Those golden days from me;
Thy voice comes strange
        O'er years of change.
How can I follow thee?
(Palgrave, quoted by Hugh Martin in *The Claims of Christ*, SCM, 1955, p. 24)

The importance of becoming like Christ

Yet in spite of the obvious problems – problems of personal failure and of cultural change – we have no liberty to drop the subject in despair. Two factors should weigh with us.

First, Christlikeness is what *God* wants to see in us. If we had to sum up in a single brief sentence what life is all about, why Jesus Christ came into this world to live and die and rise, and what God is up to in the long-drawn-out historical process both BC and AD, it would be difficult to find a more succinct explanation than this: *God is making human beings more human by making them more like Christ.* For God created us in his own image in the first place, which we then spoiled and skewed by our disobedience. Now he is busy restoring it. And he is doing it by making us like Christ, since Christ is both perfect man and perfect image of God (Colossians 1:15; 2 Corinthians 4:4).

This, at least, is the account which the apostles of Christ give us in the New Testament of God's unfolding purpose. It was his purpose in *predestination*. There is no need at this point to become distracted by the theological and moral questions which the doctrine of divine predestination raises. It is sufficient to note the stated objective of God's predestinating grace: 'those God foreknew he also predestined to be conformed to the likeness of his Son, that he might be the first-born among many brothers' (Romans 8:29). The same purpose may be discerned in the beginning of the Christian life which is commonly called *conversion* from the human perspective (as we turn from sin to Christ) and *regeneration* from the divine (as he gives us new birth and new life). What is the fundamental character of this experience? It is that we put on a new nature which is 'created to be like God in true righteousness and holiness' or 'renewed...in the image of its Creator' (Ephesians 4:24; Colossians 3:10).

The continuing of the Christian life has the same essential character and purpose as its beginning. For it is the maturing of the new-born child, the bursting of a bud into blossom, the ripening of a seed into fruit. The process of growth into holiness we usually call *sanctification*. But what is holiness except Christlikeness? We are to learn to 'live just as Jesus Christ lived' (1 John 2:6, GNB). And the end, which we often refer to as *heaven*? What do we know about that? Not much, the apostles say. The final glory is far beyond our comprehension. 'What we will be has not yet been made known.' Yet, though we do not know in any detail what our final and glorified state will be like, we do know this: 'we know that when he appears, we shall be like him, for we shall see him as he is'. This is John's statement (1 John 3:2). Paul's is similar: 'Just as we have borne the likeness of the earthly man, so shall we bear the likeness of the man from heaven' (1 Corinthians 15:49, cf. Philippians 3:21).

The fashion among contemporary scholars is to discern a dozen different theologies in the New Testament. In contrast, do you not find this convergence of texts exciting? God's whole purpose, conceived in a past eternity, being worked out for and in his people in history, to be completed in the glory to come, may be encapsulated in this single concept: *God intends to make us like Christ*. Whether we are thinking about eternal predestination or initial conversion or continuing sanctification or final glorification, the same theme stands out. At each stage there is a reference to the 'image' or 'likeness' of Jesus Christ. The fulness of salvation is conformity to him. Wisdom is often heard from the mouths of babes and sucklings. It is found in the children's chorus:

> Like Jesus, like Jesus
> I want to be like Jesus.
>   I love him so
>   I want to grow
> Like Jesus day by day.

There is a second argument for the great importance of Christlikeness. Christlikeness is not only what God wants to see in his people, but also what *the watching world* wants to see. For the name of Jesus Christ is constantly on Christian lips. We speak of him, sing of him, pray to him, bear witness to him. Therefore the world has a right to see in us this Jesus of whom we talk so much. In fact, nothing hinders the testimony of the Christian church more than the wide gap between our claims and our performance, between the Christ we proclaim verbally and the Christ we present visually.

This is true everywhere, but never more dramatically so than in countries in which a non-Christian culture prevails. In such situations the difference between those who profess to follow Jesus and those who do not should be startlingly evident. When it is, people are attracted to Christ. When it is not, they are repelled. Take India as an example, and these experiences of the late Dr Stanley Jones, the American Methodist missionary. 'A penetrating but kindly old philosopher of India, Bara Dada, the brother of Dr Rabindranath Tagore' once said to Stanley Jones: 'Jesus is ideal and wonderful, but you Christians – you are not like him.' On another occasion a Hindu lecturer on educational subjects, addressing an audience of educationalists in South India, said: 'I see that a good many of you here are Christians. Now this is not a religious lecture, but I would like to pause long enough to say that, if you Christians would live like Jesus Christ, India would be at your feet tomorrow' (*The Christ of the Indian Road* by E. Stanley Jones, 1925. Hodder and Stoughton, 1926, pp. 141–2).

It would be a mistake to suppose, however, that the Christlikeness of Christians is necessary only in countries of Hindu, Buddhist or Moslem culture. It is urgently needed in so-called Christian countries as well. Wherever Christ is named, people expect to see him. Whoever names him has a responsibility to resemble and reflect him. In a lecture given in New York City a few years ago Cardinal Suenens laid emphasis on this:

What men are waiting for from the church, whether they realize it or not, is that the church of today show them the Gospel. Our contemporaries want to meet Christ who is alive today; they want to see him with their eyes and touch him with their hands. Like those pilgrims who approached Philip one day, they say to us, 'we want to see Jesus'. Our contemporaries want a meeting face to face with Christ. The challenge for us as Christians is that they demand to see Christ in each one of us; they want us to reflect Christ as clearly as a pane of glass transmits the rays of the sun. Whatever is opaque and besmirched in us disfigures the face of Christ in the church. What the unbeliever reproaches us with is not that we are Christians, but that we are not Christian enough: that is the tragedy.
(*The Future of the Christian Church* by Archbishop Ramsey and Cardinal Suenens, SCM, 1971, p. 15)

Having considered the need for Christlikeness, because of both the purpose of God and the expectation of the world, we are ready to learn from Scripture how we are intended to grow into it. Here is Paul's teaching to the Corinthian Christians:

And we, who with unveiled faces all reflect the Lord's glory, are being transformed into his likeness with ever-increasing glory, which comes from the Lord, who is the Spirit. (2 Corinthians 3:18)

What is immediately apparent from this text is that it contains references to both 'the Lord' and 'the Spirit', that is, to the second and third persons of the Trinity. Indeed, it relates the work of the Spirit to the person of the Son. When interpreted in its context, it indicates that two of the Holy Spirit's chief delights are to show us the glory of Christ and to change us into the image of Christ.

The Holy Spirit shows us the glory of Jesus Christ

Paul is reminding his Corinthian readers what happened when Moses came down from Mount Sinai with the ten commandments. His face shone with heavenly glory because he had been speaking with the Lord God (Exodus 34:29–35). The people looked at him, saw his shining face, and were afraid to go near him. So Moses covered his face with a veil of some kind, lest they should be dazzled or frightened by the glory, and (Paul adds) lest they should see it fade away (verse 13). Because of the veil, therefore, the glory of the Lord was hidden from them. Moses removed it only when he went into the holy tent of the Lord's presence to speak to him.

The apostle sees this as a picture of the situation in his day. The glory of the Lord was still hidden from people. They could not see it. This was not because the apostles veiled the gospel, for they did not. They were 'not like Moses' (verse 13) who veiled the glory. On the contrary, they were 'very bold' (verse 12) in proclaiming the gospel of God's glory openly. The reason people could not see was not, therefore, because the gospel was veiled but because there was a veil covering their own hearts and minds. It was this which prevented them from seeing the glory of God in Jesus Christ, whether they were Jews or Gentiles.

He begins with Jewish unbelievers:

¹⁴But their minds were made dull, for to this day the same veil remains when the old covenant is read. It has not been removed, because only in Christ is it taken away. ¹⁵Even to this day when Moses is read, a veil covers their hearts. ¹⁶But whenever anyone turns to the Lord, the veil is taken away. ¹⁷Now the Lord is the Spirit, and where the Spirit of the Lord is, there is freedom.
(2 Corinthians 3:14–17)

The repetition in verses 14 and 15 is emphatic:

Verse 14: *'To this day the same veil remains when the old covenant is read.'*

Verse 15: *'To this day when Moses is read, a veil covers their hearts.'*

Their problem is not ignorance, but blindness. They read the Old Testament, but they do not see Jesus Christ as the Person to whom it bears witness. So the blindfolding veil remains, because 'only in Christ (i.e. only when he is seen and acknowledged as scripture's fulfilment) is it taken away' (verse 14), and only when 'anyone turns to the Lord the veil is taken away' (verse 16), as in the case of Moses. Now 'the Lord' in that quotation from Exodus 34, Paul continues (verse 17), is 'the Spirit', and 'where the Spirit of the Lord is, there is freedom'. For the Holy Spirit is the Spirit of Jesus Christ. It is he and only he who liberates people from their spiritual blindness by

A detail from **Ecce Homo** by Richard Westall.
The painting, presented by King George IV in 1824, hangs at the front of All Souls, Langham Place, London (see p. 98).
Photograph: Peter Wyart

revealing to them the glory of Jesus.

What is true of unbelieving Jews is equally true of unbelieving Gentiles. Paul does not discriminate between them. Blindness is the cause of unbelief, whoever the unbeliever may be. He goes on: 'if our Gospel is veiled, it is veiled to those who are perishing. The god of this age [i.e. the devil] has blinded the minds of unbelievers, so that they cannot see the light of the gospel of the glory of Christ, who is the image of God' (2 Corinthians 4:3,4).

These are solemn words. People are perishing in their blindness, Paul writes. This is not because we veil the gospel. We do not. On the contrary, we refuse to 'distort the word of God' but rather proclaim it 'by setting forth the truth plainly' (verse 2). Again, 'we preach...Jesus Christ as Lord' (verse 5). So, he stresses, if people are perishing in unbelief, it is not because we hide or distort or manipulate the gospel, but because the devil has blinded their minds to keep them from seeing it. This makes the preaching of the gospel the more urgent. For it is through the fearless proclamation of the good news that God utters his creative command 'let there be light'. Only then does 'the light of the knowledge of the glory of God in the face of Christ' (verse 6) stream into darkened human hearts.

As a result of this gracious, creative initiative of God (if we may return now to 2 Corinthians 3:18), we all have an 'unveiled face'. We are not like Moses who veiled his face. We are not like unbelieving Jews who have a veil covering their hearts. We are not like unbelieving Gentiles whose minds have been blinded by Satan. No, 'we all' have 'unveiled faces' – all of us. It is a characteristic of all God's people – whether Jews or Gentiles, black or white, young or old, educated or uneducated – that the blindfold has been stripped from our minds, that the scales have fallen from our eyes, and that we have seen Jesus. With unveiled face and opened eyes we gaze upon the glory of the Lord. On Mount Sinai only *one* man, Moses, saw the glory of the Lord Jehovah. Today *all* God's people see the glory of the Lord Jesus.

It is not certain how the first verse in verse 18 should be translated. Since *katoptron* is a 'mirror', the verb *katoptrizō* may mean either to 'reflect like a mirror' or to 'behold as in a mirror'. Translations and commentators divide on this issue. The New English Bible, J. B. Phillips, the Good News Bible and the New International Version render the word 'reflect', but the AV and RSV 'behold'. Personally, I prefer the latter as more suited to the context. It also seems to me that the 'mirror' image indicates what kind of contemplation of Christ's glory is in mind. Not yet do we behold his glory directly. Not yet do we see him 'face to face'. For this we have to wait until he comes (see e.g. John 17:24; 1 Corinthians 13:12; 1 John 3:2; Revelation 22:4). Meanwhile, although we see him 'with unveiled faces', we him 'as in a mirror'. We were not alive when he lived on earth. Most of us do not claim to have had visions or dreams in which he has appeared to us. Instead, the 'mirror' in which we have seen the historic Jesus is the New Testament in which the apostolic witness to him has been for ever definitively preserved.

What, then, is he like? this Jesus of the New Testament apostolic testimony? this Jesus whose glory is here displayed before our wondering eyes? this Jesus who is set forth as our example, that we should be 'transformed into his likeness' and become 'like him'? Only the briefest sketch of him can be attempted.

First, Jesus Christ our model is the one who 'emptied himself' and 'humbled himself'. That is, he emptied himself of rule, and humbled himself to serve. He refused to cling to the prerogatives of his own eternal deity. He laid aside his heavenly majesty. He renounced his status and his privileges. The apostles lay much stress on the humility and the generosity of Jesus as displayed in the Incarnation, and they set these things before us for our imitation. 'We...ought...not to please ourselves....For even Christ did not please himself.' 'See that you also excel in the grace of giving...For you know the grace of our Lord Jesus Christ, that though he was rich, yet for your sakes he became poor, so that you through his poverty might become rich.' Again, 'your attitude should be the same as that of Christ Jesus, who...emptied himself [RSV]...and...humbled himself...' (Romans 15:1, 3; 2 Corinthians 8:7,9 and Philippians 2:5,7,8).

Secondly, Jesus Christ our model is the one who served other people in their need. Self-humbling without the service of others may be but an empty gesture. Christ humbled himself to serve. He had not come to be served, he said, but to serve. And serve he did, responding with unfailing compassion to human need in its bewildering diversity. He fed the hungry, healed the sick, comforted the sad, befriended the dropout, forgave the sinner, raised the dead, and announced good news to the poor. He even assumed a slave's apron, washed his disciples' feet and said: 'Now that I, your Lord and Teacher, have washed your feet, you also should wash one another's feet. I have set you an example that you should do as I have done for you.' Now he sends us into the world, just as he was sent into the world, to witness and serve like him, and to respond in compassionate sensitivity to human need (Mark 10:45; John 13:14, 15; John 20:21; 1 John 3:16).

Thirdly, Jesus Christ our model is the one who loved his enemies. He taught his followers not to repay evil for evil, or even to desire revenge, but to love their enemies, pray for their persecutors and do good to those who wanted to do harm to them. And Jesus practised what he preached. As Peter put it later: 'If you suffer for doing good and you endure it, this is commendable before God. To this you were called, because Christ suffered for you, leaving you an example, that you should follow in his steps. "He committed no sin, and no deceit was found in his mouth." When they hurled their insults at him, he did not retaliate; when he suffered, he made no threats. Instead, he entrusted himself to him who judges justly' (1 Peter 2:20–23; see also Romans 15:7; Ephesians 5:2; Colossians 3:13).

Fourthly, Jesus Christ our model is the one who trusted and obeyed God. He 'learned obedience from what he suffered' and 'became obedient to death, even death on a cross'. Instead of taking revenge, he committed himself and his cause to the Judge of all humankind. When savagely tempted by the devil to distrust or disobey God, he strenuously resisted. From beginning to end his life and ministry were marked by trust and obedience (Hebrews 5:8; Philippians 2:8, cf. Romans 5:19; 1 Peter 2:23; Matthew 4:1–11).

This is the Jesus whose glory the Holy Spirit shows us in the mirror of the New Testament. He emptied himself, he served others, he loved his enemies, he trusted and obeyed God. Humility, self-sacrificial service, non-retaliation and forgiveness, faith and obedience – these are the outstanding characteristics of Jesus of Nazareth, the Jesus we are to imitate. Having seen his glory, we are to reflect it.

The Holy Spirit changes us into the likeness of Jesus Christ

We must not fail to notice how the two verbs in 2 Corinthians 3:18 relate to one another. At the beginning of the verse we are described as 'beholding' (RSV) the glory of the Lord; at the end of the verse we 'are being changed' into it. Moreover, as the verb changes, so does the historical event to which Paul is alluding. For he seems to be thinking now not of Moses on Mount Sinai whose shining face reflected the Lord's glory, but of Jesus on the Mount of Transfiguration whose face, skin and clothing all shone with a radiance which came not from without but from within. He was 'transfigured' before them, Matthew and Mark write, and Paul uses the very same verb here (*metamorphoō*). 'We are being transfigured', he says, using the present continuous tense of the verb, 'from one degree of glory to another' (RSV). That is, the glory of Jesus Christ which we behold, and into which we are being changed, does not fade like the glory on the face of Moses, or even like the glory of the temporarily transfigured Jesus. On the contrary, it increases from one degree to the next.

We must be careful how we understand this, and avoid the opposite extremes into which sections of the church have regularly fallen. On the one hand, there is no perfectionism here. For however holy or Christlike Christians may become, they are still in the condition of 'being changed'. Not till Christ comes will any of his followers be fully like him, for not till then will we see him as he is. On the other hand, there is no complacency here either. For we 'are being' transformed. We have not come to a standstill in our Christian growth. We have not got stuck in the mud. Our Christian life is not like a stagnant pool. No, we are being continuously changed into Christ's likeness, and should expect to go on being changed until our death or Christ's coming signals the moment of final transformation. Thus the Christian life is a progressive 'metamorphosis' into Christ's image, a steady, ongoing, unceasing process of becoming more like him.

How does it happen? Paul goes on that this 'comes from the Lord, who is the Spirit'. The same Lord whose glory we behold is himself changing us into his image and likeness. We are being made like him by him. It is the Lord Jesus who makes us like the Lord Jesus. And he does it by his Holy Spirit. For the Holy Spirit is the Spirit of Jesus, and in this text for the second time Paul makes the identification. 'Now the Lord is the Spirit' (verse 17) and this 'comes from the Lord, who is the Spirit' (verse 18). Sanctification is the process by which we are being transformed into the image of Christ by the Spirit of Christ.

But again we ask: how? Paul does not give a direct answer to this question here as he does elsewhere. Yet already in verse 3 of the chapter he has referred to the inward work of the Spirit. For there he has likened the Corinthian Christians to a letter from Christ which had been written 'not with ink but with the Spirit of the living God', 'not on tablets of stone [like the Ten Commandments] but on tablets of human hearts'. In other words, Jesus Christ by his Spirit is writing God's moral law on the hearts of his people; it is like a letter of commendation which everybody can read. Paul is referring to the inward, sanctifying work of the Holy Spirit which becomes visible in Christlikeness of character, and without which Christlikeness is impossible.

This is certainly what we need. We know from both Scripture and experience that self-centredness is deeply ingrained in our fallen nature. A seventeenth-century Scottish author named James Durham expressed it well but quaintly when he published a booklet in 1686 entitled 'The great corruption of subtile self, discovered, and driven from its lurking holes, in seven sermons'. Original sin having made us all thus subtly and strongly self-centred, we may be quite sure that Christ-centredness and Christ-likeness will never be attained by our own unaided efforts. How can self drive out self? As well expect Satan to drive out Satan! For we are not interested in skin-deep holiness, in a merely external resemblance to Jesus Christ. We are not satisfied by a superficial modification of behaviour patterns in conformity to some Christian sub-culture which expects this, commands that and prohibits the other. No, what we long for is a deep inward change of character, resulting from a change of nature and leading to a radical change of conduct. In a word we want to be *like Christ*, and that thoroughly, profoundly, entirely. Nothing less than this will do.

But how? For the third time we ask the same question. William

Temple helped people in his day to grasp the Christian way of holiness by drawing an analogy between Shakespeare and Jesus, and declaring the impossibility of copying either. How could we ever write plays like Shakespeare's? How could we ever live a life like Christ's? It is impossible. The very suggestion is ludicrous. Ah, but if the genius of Shakespeare were able to enter us, then we could write plays like him, and if the Spirit of Jesus were able to enter us, then we could live a life like him. The good news is that although we cannot have the genius of Shakespeare we can have the Spirit of Jesus! The Christian way of holiness is not that we struggle to live like Jesus but that he by his Spirit comes to live in us. The secret is not 'imitation' (Christians imitating Christ's live) so much as 'reproduction' (Christ reproducing his life through us). It is not just that we see the glory of Jesus by the illumination of the Holy Spirit, but that we are being changed into the image of Jesus by the indwelling power of the Holy Spirit.

It is appropriate that we should conclude this meditation by affirming the indispensable necessity of the work of the Holy Spirit. For he is the Spirit of Christ, and his ministry focuses on Christ. He shows us the glory of Christ and changes us into the image of Christ. That is to say, the Holy Spirit is a Christ-centred Spirit. So if we wish to be Christ-centred Christians (as we should wish), then it is the Holy Spirit we need. We must come daily and continuously to Jesus Christ to ask for the fulness of his Spirit. Only then will he reveal Christ to us and form Christ in us. Only then shall we begin at least to approximate to the Christ-centred, Christ-like Christians we long – for the sake of his glory – to be.

Conclusion

A Christian is, we have seen, somebody personally related to Jesus Christ. Christianity without Christ is a chest without a treasure, a frame without a portrait, a corpse without breath. Christ comes to each of us with an individual summons: 'Come to me', 'follow me'. And the Christian life begins as, however hesitantly and falteringly, we respond to his call. Then as we start following him, we discover to our increasing and delighted surprise, that a personal relationship to Christ is a many-sided, many-coloured, many-splendoured thing. We find that he is our mediator and our foundation, our life-giver and our lord, the secret and the goal of our living, our lover and our model. Or, bringing together the prepositions we have been considering, we learn that to be a Christian is to live our lives through, on, in, under, with, unto, for and like Jesus Christ. Each preposition indicates a different kind of relationship, but in each case Christ himself is at the centre.

There is so much in the world today which threatens to seduce the church from faithfulness to her heavenly bridegroom, and to distract her from essentials. I do not doubt that Paul, were he here in person today, would address to us the very same words that he addressed to the Christians in Corinth: 'I am afraid that just as Eve was deceived by the serpent's cunning, your minds may somehow be led astray from your sincere and pure devotion to Christ' (2 Corinthians 11:3). We all need constantly to be brought back to this personal devotion, this 'one thing' which Martha had not learned but Mary had, and which Jesus said was not to be taken away from her (Luke 10:38–42).

Those of us who are pastors would do well to heed the admonition of Richard Baxter in his great work *The Reformed Pastor* (1656): 'if we can but teach *Christ* to our people, we teach them all'.

And all of us, whether pastors or people, need to recover something of the passion for Christ which has animated the saints in every age. I take two Scottish divines as my example. Andrew Bonar wrote at the end of his sketch of Samuel Rutherford: 'Oh for his insatiable desires Christward! Oh for ten such men in Scotland to stand in the gap! – men who all day long find nothing but Christ to rest in, whose very sleep is pursuing after Christ in dreams' (*Andrew A. Bonar: Diary and Life*, edited by Marjory Bonar, Banner of Truth, 1960, pp. 288 and xv).

If Christ were at the centre like that, an ailing church would quickly regain its health, and ailing Christians their vitality. For the principal thing is simply this, that we *focus on Christ*.